Praise for The Teacher Within

"World class schools are vibrant, creative and inspirational environments to learn and work in. No matter where in the world, regardless of gender, age, ethnicity or curriculum studied, it is paramount that teachers, support staff, leaders and governors are aware, trained and encouraged to be vigilant for well-being issues; and that proactive activities like mindfulness and happiness habits are recognised as having positive benefits for all connected to the school life. Collectively, we need to do our utmost to continue to research and improve our understanding in this area so that our profession can deliver outstanding practice. So, as you prepare to enjoy reading this insightful book, please take a precious moment to always remember to… know yourself, be yourself and look after yourself!"

Colin Bell,

Council of British International Schools (COBIS)
CEO

"Educators around the world know the significance of teachers in influencing the academic and social development of students in their care.
Research regularly demonstrates that teachers are the single most important factor, accounting for nearly one-third of the variance in student's achievement. Enlightened Teachers focus on the development of 21st century skills in their students. But, as *The Teacher Within* reminds us, the most effective educators first develop, harness and apply their 21st century skills in their own teaching and learning practices. Susan and Simona have taken their shared passion for education to create a knowledgeable and thoughtful guide to help educators maintain, or indeed recapture, their enthusiasm for making the difference that we know they can, to the lives of their students in a way that will have a lasting positive impact."

Roderick D Fraser AM

Chairman
Round Square Board of Trustees

"This book will be ideal to support teachers, parents, and students in schools that are seeking to find their way forward to improving our educational system around the world. It is a clear, understandable and practical guide to transform our thinking about what is needed at this time if we wish to produce better learning outcomes. Humanizing learning will help create a more just and sustainable society that we say we want. I highly recommend this to all the stakeholders in education."

Ward Mailliard

Values in World Thought Program
Mount Madonna School

"I recommend with full confidence The Teacher Within, a revolutionary text because it acknowledges, with authenticity and deep understanding, that the world and each of us are in a profound emotional and spiritual process of transformation. I had the chance to be one of the witnesses of the transformation of one of the authors, Simona Baciu, a woman with an incredible power of change, an inspiration for teachers who will read this book."

Domnica Petrovai

CEO/Founder
MIND EDUCATION & HEALTH

"This outstanding book should reach each and every teacher, as it will touch their soul, it will keep them going, and it will teach them to fly. Giving teachers the support they need to pursue their noble calling is at least as important as giving students access to education. The Teacher Within is effective and instrumental in providing the educators with such support, by bringing teachers' well-being into focus and offering a brilliantly crafted and carefully paced inner development program for teachers. The Teacher Within is truly transformational not only for the teachers but, through them, for students, schools, education systems, and, in the end, for our world."

Irina Anghel-Enescu,
Member of the Academy of Global Teacher Prize

"This book serves as a fantastic guide for bringing the power of mindfulness into the profession of teaching. Teaching is one of the most rewarding professions, but also one of the most demanding. This book offers simple, ready-to-use, and evidence-based mindfulness techniques to help educators see beyond the walls of the classroom and find their core values. Reading this book, you will discover that, if you want to grow, if you want to make a difference, become a mindful teacher."

Dr. Hedi Hoka
MBSR expert

"Often, in times of dilemma, we have to get our moral compass out and discover what our own advice may be. Just like the subtle signs of stress or exhaustion, it takes patience and practice to take a breath and finally listen to the teacher within."

Owen McComasky
Lower primary school teacher

"The teacher within is about understanding oneself, other people and the world around all of us so that we can all guide each other, share and enjoy our lives."

Jim Geary
English teacher

"Simona Baciu and Susan Shapiro offer important insights for us, as human beings and specifically as teachers. Teachers play a key role in developing a healthy atmosphere in their own classroom and an equally important role in creating core values within our societies. Beyond hard skills, teachers transmit the soft skills they embody. So who they are matters! Through a personal development model based on self -awareness and resilience training, Simona and Susan offer teachers a support for healthy personal development, with an expected impact on their students. Within this book, we as teachers find a safe way to access our inner resources for the sake of not only our students but also of ourselves. I wish all of us a beautiful Transformation trip through the ARAT model landscape!"

Valérie Cioloş-Villemin
Authorized mindfulness stress reduction trainer- MBSR®

"Any self-discovery enriches our life perspective and brings us to a totally new space of living a fulfilled life. When mindfulness, resilience, and authenticity become accessible to a teacher, the benefits are multiplied and will flow to their thousands of students and beyond. Once the access to the teacher within has been achieved, the world will be blessed with rounded people, as our children will discover the treasure that lies within them and will learn how to express that fully. I truly believe the tools Susan and Simona provide in the book will bring peace, understanding, and harmony in many lives and communities and add significant value to the teaching profession."

Anca Harasim
Executive Director
American Chamber of Commerce in Romania
Member of the AmCham Network

The

TEACHER WITHIN

....

A Mindful Journey Toward Well-Being For Teachers In The 21St Century

Susan Shapiro & Simona Baciu

the TEACHER WITHIN

ISBN: 979-8-9860574-2-2

Illustrations design: Ana-Maria Huluban

Design: Mihai-Vlad Guță

Editor: Cristina I. Marine, PhD, University of Maryland University College, USA

Printed by: Tapestry Intergenerational Educational Foundation (TIEF)

Original printing: 2018, revisions 2019 and 2025

InIm Institute is a non-governmental organization dedicated to the socio-emotional development of young people and professionals in education and mental health, offering relevant solutions for contemporary challenges. With a strong foundation in research and speciality studies, the organization develops training programs and courses tailored to the ever-changing educational and social context. These initiatives are designed to address needs identified at both national and international levels, ensuring a lasting impact in various communities.

Our main goal is to build an interdisciplinary community where every member feels a sense of belonging, fostering personal and professional growth.

Our programs promote values such as emotional intelligence, resilience, wisdom, and solidarity, aimed at reducing stress and encouraging well-being and mental health.

The purpose of the TIEF is (1) to promote and support the education empowering wellbeing of children, youth, and adults, and its creative content, literacy, peer connections, to weave together creativity, inspiration and belonging, and (2) to support and conduct non-partisan research, education, and informational activities to increase public awareness of mental health, not to limit the ability of the Corporation to carry out any other charitable, literary, and educational purposes. For more information - see: www.tief.info

This book is dedicated to

Noah

Jake

Zachary

Annie

Liam

Ilinca

Petra

Vlad

and to all the children in the world.

They deserve guidance and inspiration from the best.

They are our future!

The Teacher's Well-being: A Conscious Journey program is based on the concepts from the book *The Teacher Within* (May 2018), written by Susan Shapiro, Vice President, Project Creator and Director of the Tapestry Intergenerational Education Foundation (TIEF), and Simona Baciu, member of TIEF and president of InIm Institute. Initially, the training program concept and the book were presented at TEDx HSMC in Hong Kong during the speech titled *Thoughts, Emotions and Seeds – An Inter-VIEW, a View of Your Inner Self,* followed by several training sessions organized for students and teachers at the University of Hong Kong, as well as for teachers at Avendale International Kindergarten Hong Kong and Education Connect Hong Kong."

CONTENTS

FOREWORD

Susan Shapiro and Simona Baciu are two long-time friends with a shared passion for education. Together, they recall the birth of the idea that eventually became *The Teacher Within*.

The story began almost three decades ago after communism had fallen across Eastern and Central Europe. In 1991, Susan Shapiro, Director of the Open Society's Health Education Program, traveled to Romania to introduce teachers to a new and innovative way of teaching and learning, something they had never experienced before.

Susan touched the life of thousands of teachers in this part of the world, and Simona Baciu was one of them. Simona was fascinated by Susan's experience and philosophy in education. In her words, "I dreamt of a time when a similar culture in education would exist in Romania." Two years later, in 1993, Simona started her pioneering project in education, Happy Kids Kindergarten, using Susan's curriculum as the foundation for teaching.

Over time, Susan and Simona's friendship evolved due to their shared passion for education. Susan is now an educator, consultant, and author of numerous books pertaining to personal development and life-skills.

Simona's kindergarten grew over the years and became Transylvania College, The Cambridge International School in Cluj, recognized nationally and internationally as an elite institute for primary and secondary education. Simona is now an educator, speaker, author, trainer, and consultant for the improvement of education in Romania and abroad.

In 2012, they chatted over a cup of coffee in Susan's kitchen in Washington, DC. Simona recalls, *"We were brainstorming the importance of keeping teachers' motivation and enthusiasm alive, through the ups and downs they face. We knew that, overcoming or embracing challenges, teachers will make a huge difference in their students' lives, guiding them to find the spark within themselves."*

Their conversation continued by phone, across the ocean and time zones. Their philosophy evolved through numerous conversations and visits and, eventually, generated the idea for Susan and Simona to write this book together.

The Teacher Within is a journey for you to look within yourself and find who you are. When you teach from the heart, you will find the power to overcome challenging times, to be there for your students no matter the circumstances, and to transform your bad days into good ones.

Teaching is a calling. Imagine the change that can occur if teachers felt fulfilled, and if they role modeled such behavior to their students. An emotionally rounded, happy teacher makes a strong positive impact on each student in every class.

INTRODUCTION

A NEW PHILOSOPHY TO DISCOVER YOUR POWER WITHIN

It was an early spring day in Transylvania when Susan and Simona were traveling together and arrived at a tiny village on the top of the mountains. They were looking for a place to freshen up and catch their breath when they saw an elderly man ploughing the rocky land. Simona asked him, "What are you up to?" He replied, "I'm preparing the land for my vegetable garden." Surprised, they looked around and all they could see was rocky mountains and evergreens. Yet, he was speaking about a vegetable garden working hard to prepare the soil.

Simona then asked, "Can you even grow vegetables here on such hard soil?" The man said, "I know what my land can do; all it takes is hard work. You are welcome to come back for cabbage soup in September!" The confident tone of his voice made Susan and Simona smile and picture the fresh cabbage soup on the table. At that moment, they knew this was a lesson to be learned.

The hard-working man driven by his strong vision became a symbol for the journey of *The Teacher Within*: when you are aware of who you are and recognize your strengths as your inner driving force, you commit to actions and accomplish your vision. This inner journey is described in four words: **Awareness**, **Recognition**, **Actions**, and **Transformation**. These words make up the acronym for a Romanian word **ARAT** [a 'r a t] which means to plough the land, make the first furrow. ARAT has become our metaphor for teachers to discover their power within, teaching from the heart to best serve their students.

Imagine the Land of **Awareness**, a fertile but seedless soil. The sun and the water give full **Recognition** and prepare the soil with love. You come along, dig deep and make the first furrow. You take **Action** and plant the seed with care. The soil, the water, and the sun nurture its growth. Sometimes the wind blows hard, and it isn't easy for the little plant to show its head. But you persist and leave your imprint in the soil, watering the plant, caring for it, and making sure it will grow. You move from the Land of Awareness into the Land of **Transformation** where the plant grows stronger thanks to your effort and commitment. This is the philosophy of *The Teacher Within*.

THE FOUR LEVELS

Many outstanding books with innovative ideas are written about teaching and schools in the 21st century. They mostly bring new concepts in education with a focus on the holistic development of children, helping them adapt to the needs and interests of a rapidly changing society.

But who is the person who is there to guide and teach these children? It is The Teacher.

Teachers of the 21st century need to be visionaries and strategists; educators with equal measures of compassion and motivation; persons who are open and willing to learn and adapt their skills, knowledge, and personalities to best impact their students.

We invite you to read *The Teacher Within* and look beyond the walls of the classroom to discover the spark that keeps your calling alive. This book is a guided journey for you to achieve balance and harmony in your body, mind, heart, and spirit. You will become aware of your body, accept your thoughts and emotions in your mind, engage in actions from the heart, and wholeheartedly commit to transformation. ARAT is the key to a mindful, resilient, and authentic teacher.

LEVEL ONE – AWARENESS

Becoming aware of yourself is the foundation of *The Teacher Within* presented in Level One. Through increased awareness of your body and senses, you experience the positive effects of mindfulness. The first ten days introduce you to breath awareness, meditation, and concentration practices. You discover the importance of concepts such as kindness, living in the "here" and "now" and choosing peace of mind.

As you proceed day by day, you will notice positive changes. You will understand more about your thoughts, emotions, and feelings. You will observe the importance of your breath and how it takes you to the present moment, giving you valuable information about your hopes and dreams. You may experience less stress and more joy in your everyday life, even in this short amount of time.

Over the first ten days, you become comfortable with the vocabulary and the techniques offered through a Daily Practice. We ask you to follow it with a "One Minute Meditation" to bolster your learning.

LEVEL TWO – RECOGNITION

Recognition, Level Two, is your journey of self-analysis to embrace your thoughts and emotions. You learn to recognize your thinking pattern, follow your intuition, and set up intentions to achieve your goals. You acknowledge your habits and your inner power to change the ones that don't serve you.

During these 20 days, regular mindfulness practices project a clear picture of your emotions and give you practical tools to manage them. At this level, you learn to transform difficult emotions into manageable opportunities, generating a positive outcome.

LEVEL THREE – ACTIONS

Through awareness and recognition of your body and mind, you have laid the foundation for the actions you need to take and fully commit to. At this level, for the next 30 days, you take practical Actions to become a mindful and resilient teacher and this guides you to build your conscious classroom.

Your actions bring beneficial routines into your classroom and into your life. They lessen your stress. Examples of these actions include: pause when you are overwhelmed, choose positive words of empowerment, form habits of positive self-talk, and stay committed to your vision.

As you become a mindful and resilient teacher, you go beyond academics toward the creation of a conscious classroom, a "class with a heart." You realize your presence cannot be separated from the context of the classroom. You are able to fulfill your students' needs. You acknowledge your students' strengths as you cultivate their love of learning, thereby creating a safe and predictable environment.

LEVEL FOUR – TRANSFORMATION

After a journey of 60 days through awareness and recognition of your body and mind, and actions taken from the heart, you move onto the path of a spiritual transformation so that you may blossom at your fullest potential. This is a holistic approach to well-being, strengthening your body, mind, heart, and spirit connection. You are now able to embrace healthy thoughts and emotions and achieve inner peace.

You notice the difference inside you as you change. You feel empowered with commitment and motivation, and you give and receive acts of love and kindness showing compassion to those around you. Your authentic voice inspires and motivates your students so their enthusiasm for learning is kept alive.

Since your brain is only 14 inches away from the heart, this transformative journey enables you to teach with your mind and your heart, as you follow the path toward the inner harmony of *The Teacher Within*.

HOW TO USE THIS BOOK

The book is designed as a 100-day journey to guide you through practices to become a mindful and resilient teacher. Each day, you read the material and complete a Daily Practice followed by a One Minute Meditation. As you work through the four levels of the ARAT philosophy, we suggest that you do the Daily One Minute Meditation anytime you want.

The Four levels of ARAT are structured into ten chapters, ten days for a chapter, with each chapter building on the previous ones and adding new concepts. Each level draws you further toward discovering *The Teacher Within*. We recommend that you spend roughly five minutes every day, reading and practicing the exercises. Do not be tempted to spend more than five minutes on the entire process. In time, you will find that small changes are powerful, sustainable, and bring large gains.

Throughout the book, you will read stories of teachers who shared their experiences and personal challenges. Their honesty, courage, and generosity in allowing us to use their quotes have enhanced our message. We have used fictitious names to protect their identity. Some quotes have been combined so that you, the reader, can sharpen your perception.

To symbolize your transformation while reading this book you will be asked to buy flower seeds, for example, zinnias, cosmos, or marigolds. On Day 91, you will plant these seeds, so that you may enjoy the growth process of your beautiful plant symbolizing your own transformational change towards reaching your full potential.

inner
peace
awareness
positive affirmations
concentration
smile
meditation
mindfulness
pause
senses
BODY
breath
awareness
see
touch
peace of mind
present moment
smell
hear
gratitude
here and now
mindful journey
self-awareness
beginning
connect to yourself

LEVEL ONE

AWARENESS

awareness

CHAPTER ONE

AWARENESS OF YOURSELF

Awareness is a journey of introspection for each of us and it has no fixed destination. The path you take in your life defines the quality of your journey. Your beliefs begin with your thoughts and you become what you believe. Becoming aware of your thoughts is the foundation of a better understanding of yourself. When you are aware of your thoughts and your beliefs, you are inviting new energy into your life. You understand yourself better; you see your strengths and weaknesses, and you know how to use them for personal growth.

As a teacher, you didn't choose a job; you followed your calling. You go to school every day for your students, to teach, inspire, and guide them. You think of them first, using all your knowledge and power to make teaching and learning an enjoyable journey. While you are focused on your duties, you might not even realize your energy resources are draining; you start feeling stressed and overwhelmed, which may eventually lead to burnout.

When was the last time you thought of yourself and your own needs? Becoming aware of who you are is not selfishness. Replenish your energy resources and regain the power to carry on, feeling enthusiastic and energetic. Take care of yourself so you can take better care of your students.

Awareness of yourself helps you manage your days better, lower the stress levels, and keep your motivation alive. Living with awareness infuses your life with multiple possibilities. It opens your mind to happiness and joy. This process begins with observing your own breath. It anchors you to the present moment, giving you an insight into your thoughts, hopes, and dreams.

Level One, Awareness, familiarizes you with new concepts, such as breath awareness, meditation, concentration, and living in the present moment.

During the first ten days, you will explore the basic concepts through different exercises and practices. To develop your awareness, we created a guideline for you to follow:

Day 1. Focus on Your Breath

Day 2. Become Aware of Your Breath

Day 3. Live in the Present Moment: "Here and Now"

Day 4. Practice Meditation

Day 5. Practice Concentration Techniques

Day 6. Choose Inner Peace

Day 7. Practice Positive Thinking

Day 8. Show Loving Kindness

Day 9. Start the Day with Gratitude

Day 10. Practice Positive Affirmations

Take a leap of faith and give yourself the chance to open a new door.

DAY 1

FOCUS ON YOUR BREATH

This chapter gives you a tool you can carry with you at all times and can be used whenever you need it. It may be the most essential tool for you to gain control over your life. This tool is your breath!

Since you took your first breath, about ten seconds after you were born, it has continued to sustain your life. As a baby and then as a child, your breath came effortlessly from your belly. But, as you matured, your breathing may have changed and moved into your chest. This makes your breath shorter and faster and can result in pressure both on your mind and body. This pressure often morphs into a state of stress and anxiety. When you know how to breathe consciously, you achieve clarity and manage to live in the present moment. You lower your anxiety, decrease your stress, and improve your mood. These positive effects occur almost instantaneously because, when you focus on your breath, you change how your body reacts to negative stimuli. Your body moves toward a state of well-being.

The way you breathe can make a huge difference in your life. Breathe consciously for a few seconds. Make sure your stomach expands when you inhale. This form of breathing allows you to become aware of the present moment. Your breath keeps harmony between your mind and your body.

Remember when you were a child, blowing up balloons! You filled them with air, watched them expand, and admired the beauty of their colorful shapes. If you deflated the balloon by suddenly letting the air out, you could see how it shrank, and the air released quickly, making the balloon bounce uncontrollably around. You may have observed that, when you let the air out gently, the balloon deflated slowly, and you had control over it. You can gain similar awareness of your breathing by imagining your stomach as the balloon, inflating and deflating it intentionally.

DAILY PRACTICE

Focus on your breath today.

Breathe in through your nose and feel the air going through your nostrils. Breathe out through your mouth and allow your body to relax. Breathe in again through your nose and notice this time the air flowing through your nostrils to fill your body. Breathe out through your mouth as you sigh. Relax your mind and body. This short breathing practice lasts for about 30 seconds. Practice it several times today.

Daily One Minute Meditation

ONE MINUTE MEDITATION FOR CHAPTER 1

Find a comfortable seated position.

Close your eyes or lower your gaze.

Rest your hands in your lap, palms up.

Breathe in through your nose and fill your lungs.

Notice the pause of fullness.

Breathe out through your mouth until you empty your lungs.

Notice the pause of emptiness.

Become aware of the need to inhale.

This is the full cycle of your breath.

Breathe in through your nose until your lungs are full.

Notice the cool air as it enters your nostrils.

Breathe out through your mouth until your lungs are empty.

Notice the warm air as it escapes your lips.

This is the full cycle of awareness in the present moment.

Smile as you slowly open your eyes!

DAY 2

BECOME AWARE OF YOUR BREATH

The pattern of your breath is usually instinctive. It's an automatic response. You breathe without thinking about your breath, and this is natural. When you focus on your breath, your mind becomes calm, you gain awareness of your personality and acknowledge your thoughts, emotions, and needs. Breath-awareness helps you to separate from your environment and become conscious of yourself, as an individual.

Breathing affects the way your mind and body work, as well as your feelings and moods. When you become aware of your breathing and practice breath-awareness, you can increase the amount of oxygen in your blood, thus improving your brain function. Improved state of clarity, higher energy, and greater teaching achievements are all benefits a teacher can gain from proper breathing practices. You will shift out of stressful and anxious states and be able to handle challenging situations, manage conflicts, and maintain your focus while you teach.

Consider this cycle. You breathe in air and feel fulfillment, and then you release the air and feel depletion. It is a cyclical process which sustains life. Inhale through your nose and exhale through your nose or your mouth, while your body relaxes. Exhalation is followed by a pause, when there is no breathing for about two seconds. Pause exists in any breathing cycle; it's a time of silence. The awareness of this pause is a simple way to quiet your mind and open up to yourself.

Becoming aware of your breathing is helpful for teachers to quiet their mind and regain clarity. When you are overwhelmed, focus on your breath and bring back your inner peace. As you breathe, become aware of the four phases of breathing:

1. Inhale (A time of complete fulfillment)

2. Pause (A time of silence)

3. Exhale (A time of complete depletion and relaxation)

4. Pause (A time of silence to quiet your mind)

As your frustrations no longer cloud your mind, you are able to look within and regain the power to go on.

Sally, a kindergarten teacher, shared her thoughts about her day.

"My day is packed and scheduled to the hilt with meetings, tasks, and deadlines. I move from one thing to the next almost automatically. I can't complete one task because I'm preparing for the next. I can't give it my full attention either. I think I am mostly on autopilot, multi-tasking all day long. Tonight I will collapse from fatigue."

Many of us are like Sally. We have more to do than we can get done! Acting on autopilot and multi-tasking is unavoidable. This is our new way of life. If your mind is occupied with everything but the current situation, it is time to become aware of the situation and change it. Focusing on your breath helps you reconnect with the present moment and regain energy to act on the current task. Thus, your brain receives more oxygen, your body relaxes, and it brings an overall calming effect to you.

DAILY PRACTICE

Find a comfortable seat. Keep your eyes open and breathe naturally for one minute. Each breath includes an inhale and an exhale. Keep count to see how many times you breathe in one minute. You might get a count of 8 to 15 deep breaths. There is no ideal number. Remember this count; it will be your personal number per minute.

Now, close your eyes or lower your gaze and begin to count each breath. When thoughts come to your mind, observe them and go back to your breath. Continue breathing and continue observing the cycle as you: Inhale, Pause, Exhale, Pause. Do this exercise for two minutes and enjoy the peace of mind you have gained.

You can practice breath awareness in the morning, or during the day, when you feel tired or stressed.

Reference to p. 6
Daily One Minute Meditation

DAY 3

LIVE IN THE PRESENT MOMENT: "HERE" AND "NOW"

The present moment is your gift in life because it is the only moment when you have absolute freedom of action. This moment is unique and it will never come back. Learn to enjoy it and make the most of it. If you live with the fears of your past, you allow the worries and anxieties to take over your mind and take away your energy. Think about how much time you've wasted by dwelling on things from the past you aren't able to change, or worrying about things you can't foresee in the future. This way of thinking will make you feel stressed and overwhelmed.

Look around you. Observe your environment and notice how you fit into it. Being mindful of where you are, what you're doing, and what is happening around you gives you the awareness of the present moment. This is when you can act on things or change them. Learning to live in the present moment – *HERE* and *NOW* – provides a greater sense of calm in your daily life. This is because there is no time other than right now. So, look around, feel your freedom. Breathe into it.

Awareness of the present trains your mind to look deeply within and to focus on what really matters. Always keep in mind that your fears come from your past and your worries are connected to your future. It's your choice how you want to live your life.

HERE is the space around you: at home, in the car, in the classroom. Where are you in this present moment?

NOW is this present moment. It will pass quickly, but it is the only moment for you right now.

The simplest way to connect with the present moment is by connecting with your breathing. Practice this simple exercise a few seconds every day to connect with the present moment:

Breathe in, be aware of your body and your environment.

Breathe out, staying aware of your body and environment.

Inhale. Exhale. Smile.

You are now in the present moment.

Let's make one distinction. Living in the present does not mean you live a carefree life without focus on responsibilities or future planning. It does not mean you do not prepare your lessons or deal with difficult decisions. You still learn from your past while living in the present moment. It means you use your time efficiently without wasting your energy, regretting what you didn't get done yesterday, or worrying about tomorrow's unknowns. Instead, you focus on solving the challenges right in front of you.

DAILY PRACTICE

Find a comfortable seat. Close your eyes and begin to focus on your breath.

Breathe deeply for one minute. Reflect on how you are right now.

For today's practice, focus on the present moment – stop and be aware of your here and now. Expand your focus to your body and anything touching your body. Notice these sensations. Expand your awareness to everything you can hear and sense.

If you experience other thoughts, it's OK.

Inhale. Exhale.

Repeat four times.

Smile when you open your eyes.

Reference to p. 6
Daily One Minute Meditation

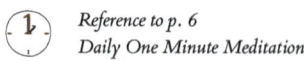

DAY 4

PRACTICE MEDITATION

Meditation is the practice in which you train your mind to relax and become still. It is the time taken out of your day when you sit or lie down in silence and focus on yourself. It teaches you to look within.

Imagine your mind is an ocean and your thoughts are the rolling waves. You worry about your students. You stress over your responsibilities. You worry about the future. Those waves are always there. Now, imagine you go beneath the waves to the silence within the ocean. You leave the turmoil and the waves, and they are temporarily gone. That's meditation. You enter a deeper state of concentration and get the chance to become aware of the present moment while you leave behind the noise and commotion of daily life.

Often, people shy away from meditation because they can't "stop thinking thoughts." However, you will always have thoughts. It is the nature of your mind to wander. When thoughts pop up, as they will, all you should do is acknowledge your thoughts and then go back to your breath. Even when you are below the waves, you can look up and see them, but you can always go back to the silence underneath.

Meditation is the most effective practice to calm your mind when you "can't stop thinking thoughts." The goal is to reach awareness of yourself and to let go of the fears and worries you hold within. Meditation opens your mind to your inner world. There are many forms of meditation you can choose from:

- One requires the repetition of a mantra, which is a word or a set of sounds with a calming effect. You repeat this word or sound over and over again and use it to anchor your mind to the present moment.

- Focusing on your breath is another form of meditation. You breathe consciously through your nose and exhale through your mouth, counting your breaths and releasing the pressure and stress of the moment.

- You can also use body scan, when you become aware of your whole body and the sensations you feel in the present moment. You pay attention to the air you inhale and how it moves through your body, relaxing each part of it.

As a teacher, you face many challenging situations. You can use any of meditation techniques described above to release the stress of the moment and look at the situation with a new perspective and an uncluttered mind.

DAILY PRACTICE

Find a comfortable place to sit. Make sure your feet are flat on the ground, your hands in your lap, your spine and torso straight, and your eyes closed or slightly open. Your mouth should be slightly open and your jaw relaxed (to relax your jaw, put your tongue behind your upper teeth).

Close your eyes and begin to focus on your breath. Be aware of the sensations you feel as the air is inhaled through your nostrils. Feel the cool flow of air when you inhale and the warmth of the flow when you exhale. You can exhale through your nose or your mouth, whichever you prefer.

Focus on the flow of your breath as you breathe in and breathe out. Continue to watch your breath. If your mind starts to wander and you are distracted, gently return to your breath, without criticizing yourself. Your thoughts are like the waves in the ocean; they come and go.

Do this exercise 10-15 times (around two minutes) and then slowly open your eyes and look around the room. Smile when you open your eyes. What do you notice?

Reference to p. 6
Daily One Minute Meditation

DAY 5

PRACTICE CONCENTRATION TECHNIQUES

While meditation is the way to an uncluttered mind, concentration is the action of a focused mind. Concentration relies on self-control, leading toward consciousness of the mind. When you concentrate, you exercise an element of control. You direct your attention to an object, to a thought or to your breath. Both your inner and outer world are involved: your mind and your environment. As you practice different concentration techniques, you develop mind-focusing skills. You gain inner power, thus lowering your fears and worries, so you can become aware of your own "teacher within."

Teachers always ask students to concentrate. But how do teachers concentrate throughout the day? What happens when you, the teacher, become distracted by outside circumstances? You want to return to the present moment and be aware of the task at hand. You cannot afford to be distracted because your focus is paramount to a healthy teaching environment. Even when you have so many other tasks, you need to stay focused and be anchored to the present moment.

Concentration can be practiced at any time. You may use simple methods to develop and improve your concentration, even during a class, when tension grows and you feel the need to reconnect. You need only a 30-second break and you can choose from any of the following simple methods:

- Pay attention to your breath.
- Focus on one object (a pen, a tree outside the window, a ray of sunlight on a piece of paper, etc.).

- Focus on the sounds surrounding you.
- Focus on numbers; count backward from 100 by twos, threes or fives.

When you notice that your students lose focus in class, you can use any of these concentration techniques so that you will regain their attention. Consider improving your concentration. Don't take it for granted. Your task list won't shorten, but you will handle it without feeling overwhelmed.

DAILY PRACTICE

Today, improve your concentration using a basic practice to become more observant of the present moment. This is something you do daily: you eat.

Take an apple. Hold it in your hand and notice its shape, color, and weight. Observe how it feels as you hold it. Notice the smooth texture with your fingers. Turn it around and see if you find any imperfections.

Now, smell it and breathe in the aroma.

Bring the apple to your mouth, close to your lips. Take a deep breath and fill your mind with awareness as you push the apple against your lips. Pause before you take a small bite.

Close your eyes to enjoy the experience.

Notice the taste and the texture but don't chew it yet.

Explore it in your mouth as you bite into it.

Do you notice thoughts coming into your mind? Do not block them. Simply allow them to flow through your mind as you focus on this bite.

Now start chewing. Focus on how it tastes.

Swallow it slowly and taste its sweetness.

Open your eyes and enjoy the next bite.

This is an exercise you can practice with your students. You may choose any other fruit.

Reference to p. 6
Daily One Minute Meditation

DAY 6

CHOOSE INNER PEACE

Inner peace is a state of mental and emotional calmness, when your mind is quiet, you don't experience worries, fears or stress, but a sense of fulfillment and happiness. Even when your day is packed with tasks, challenges and noise, leading to stress and anxiety, you can choose inner peace. When your mind is cluttered and you feel like you have a storm inside your head, you can become aware of these distractions and recognize the need for quiet time, to find your inner peace and reconnect with yourself.

There are several ways you can reach your inner peace: you can sit quietly with a cup of coffee or tea; you can look out of the window and enjoy your view; you might take a walk in the school yard or sit on a bench, clearing your mind. This stillness increases your sense of peace. It can be felt by living in a state of presence, connected to yourself. When you choose inner peace, you can unclutter your mind, calm the storm rising in your mind, and allow constructive thoughts to arise. Can you think of such peaceful moments? If you choose peace of mind, no matter the situation, any concern will feel lighter and easier to solve.

Let's take a look at Owen's story, an elementary school teacher. Owen loves teaching. He is a dedicated teacher, but there are days when his students are more energetic and disturb the class. He resonates with their energy and feels the same as they do. Owen looked for solutions to bring back a peaceful atmosphere in the classroom. He created the 'Peace of Mind Jar.' Here's how he described it: "The jar is like a snow-globe, filled with water and glitter. I brought it into in the classroom and explained to my students how it is similar to our mind. The glitter represents our thoughts, worries and fears in our mind. When the jar settles out, the glitter goes down and the water that is like our mind becomes clear. Sometimes our mind has to deal with too many thoughts and the words and actions we take can be harmful to others. When we quiet our mind, our thoughts settle down, like the glitter in the jar. We think, talk, and act differently."

Owen - "Peace of Mind Jar."

If your mind is cluttered and often filled with disturbing thoughts, over time, it leads to stress and anxiety both for you and for your students. You can reduce the stress by simply choosing inner peace and by appreciating the present moment. You have free will. No one can make you think something you don't want to think! You are in the best position to say: "I choose peace of mind."

DAILY PRACTICE

Think about a recent challenging situation. On a scale of 1 to 5, rank the level of stress you feel as you think about this situation. (1 not stressed; 5 very stressed).

Think about how this situation annoyed you. Think about why you are feeling so challenged by it. Go through the experience as if you were experiencing it right now. Yes, you can even get angry as you think about it.

Now, think again of this situation as an opportunity for you to grow. Think about it in relation to your own well-being. Choose your thoughts and for this moment, choose peace of mind.

Reference to p. 6
Daily One Minute Meditation

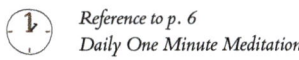

DAY 7

PRACTICE POSITIVE THINKING

The most powerful force in the world is the thought. Everything you do and say begins with your thoughts. They are the driving force of your actions and the tools you use to influence others. If your mind is set for thinking positive thoughts, they can empower you to accomplish wonderful things. On the other hand, if you let negative thoughts overwhelm you, those can crush your dreams and cause you pain and suffering.

An average brain may have between 12,000 – 60,000 thoughts per day. Of those, 80% could be negative, and 95% may be repetitive thoughts from yesterday. This estimate comes from research conducted by the National Science Foundation on daily human thoughts.

A Japanese scientist, Masaru Emoto, conducted an experiment in an elementary school to see the effect words have on the structure of water. Emoto asked the students to talk to the water, and, then, he interpreted the outcome. The results may surprise you. The water exposed to positive speech and positive thoughts turned into visually pleasing crystals, when frozen. On the other hand, negative words produced ugly frozen crystal formations. His experiment proved how powerful our words and thoughts really are. Think positive thoughts and form beautiful crystals!

Estimate your daily negative thoughts. If they are even close to 80%, it is an uphill battle to reduce them. When negative thinking is part of your vocabulary, those words create your internal image and the external response you show to others. Don't blame yourself or feel guilty. You have developed a vocabulary over the years and, most likely, you are unaware of its impact. You may even use the same words over and over again without realizing the negative impact they have on your life.

Certain words trigger positive thinking and positive statements. Positive expressions include: I can do this; anything is possible; I am thankful. In contrast, certain words trigger negative thinking and negative statements: "I cannot do this; this is impossible; this will never work out." Using mindfulness practices such as breath awareness and meditation can help you become aware of the way you think and direct your thinking pattern toward positive thoughts.

DAILY PRACTICE

Identify the way you think and how often your words reflect negative thoughts. Once you become aware of this, you can enjoy the benefits of positive thinking.

Take a piece of paper at the beginning of the school day and tear off a small bit (as much as you can pinch with two fingers) each time you have a negative thought or say a negative word. Track this for a couple of hours. How much paper is left at the end of the second hour?

What can you do to create more positive thoughts?

Reference to p. 6
Daily One Minute Meditation

DAY 8

SHOW LOVING KINDNESS

As we discussed yesterday, reducing negative thoughts and increasing the number of positive thoughts can have beneficial effects on your life. Let's go further today. You can combine love and kindness and move into self-realization. Begin with a sense of loving kindness directed inwards. Give yourself love and kindness today. Practice small acts of kindness toward yourself and toward your students.

Read Elizabeth's words showing loving kindness to her students. "You can create a supportive environment in your classroom when you practice loving kindness. It is crucial for your students to learn to be kind. They may not remember the material you teach them, but they will remember you. You show loving kindness by listening carefully to what each student says, smile when they walk into the room and use positive body language to make them feel secure. You use words to build their self-esteem. You don't interrupt them before they have finished what they want to say. Treat them just like you want to be treated – with the utmost respect and admiration."

Think about what makes you a loving and kind person. What would those closest to you say about how you show love and kindness? Recognize this love within yourself before you can share it with anyone else. It starts within you and you can project it to your environment.

Awareness of yourself, your thoughts, words, and actions will support you when you teach with love and kindness. You become a role model to your students, and they will learn from you that kindness is the foundation of a good attitude for building meaningful relationships.

DAILY PRACTICE

Reflect on your teaching and the way you want to inspire your students, beyond sharing academic knowledge. Take responsibility of your attitude and your statements. Now re-read Elizabeth's note through your own perspective. Substitute the word you with the word I: Instead of "You can create a supportive environment," say: "I can create a supportive environment." Transform her words into your own and make them your responsibility.

Reference to p. 6
Daily One Minute Meditation

DAY 9

START THE DAY WITH GRATITUDE

It's amazing how different your world can look when you start the day with gratitude! You fill your mind with positive thoughts, focus on possibilities, and set the tone for the day. When you choose gratitude to direct your mind, there is no room for fear and guilt.

When you practice gratitude, your mood improves. You gain a new outlook on life. You value your life the way it is and you focus on the positive aspects. Instead of thinking about what you don't have, you concentrate on things you have and for which you are thankful. This seems fairly simple, but it takes regular practice. Gratitude gives you the opportunity to appreciate the present moment and it is a natural extension of mindfulness.

Life brings good days and bad days, and ups and downs. You may be exhausted after a day with your students or you might feel sad when you become ill, or angry when someone does an injustice to you. However, when you focus on gratitude and on things you can be thankful for, you will bring positive energy into your life. It brings you joy even for brief moments. Gratitude saves you from staying trapped with negative thoughts and emotions and allows you to move past anger or sadness into positive and powerful thoughts.

Look around you and identify those things in your immediate environment you are thankful for. Be grateful for what you have – for your health, your family, your job, and your students. Even if they are not perfect, you have them and you can count on them. You can always find ways to improve what you have instead of focusing on what you're missing. Once you form the habit of gratitude, you will find solutions to fulfill your needs and live a more meaningful life. Make gratitude a habit!

Over time, your gratitude awareness will give you the overflowing feeling that you have enough. You start to share this gratitude with others and find you have more to be grateful for than you could have ever imagined.

Let's see how Brenda made gratitude her life skill. Brenda is a secondary school science teacher. She shared her experience with us: "I am passionate about teaching and I care for my students. This, however, makes me worry a lot about the way I teach, or the way my students master the concepts. I can't stop thinking about how they will do in their exams at the end of the school year. This constant worrying overwhelms me. One day, I was talking to Elena, a fellow teacher, sharing my thoughts. Elena used to be in a similar situation, before she started to observe her thoughts and make a change. She realized that worrying wasn't helping her become a better teacher. She started to focus on the opportunities in her profession, especially on making a difference in her students' lives. She created a statement for herself, saying that she was grateful to be with her students, to teach them and learn from them every day. I decided to try this way of thinking and adopted it. I did my best not to worry continuously, and I started practicing gratitude."

When you cultivate the habit of gratitude, you add happiness to your life. You will feel good about yourself and about others.

DAILY PRACTICE

Spend two minutes today to meditate on gratitude. Identify and state what you are grateful for. The more specific you are, the more genuine your gratitude becomes. You may consider one of the following practices:

1. When you wake up, be grateful for three things you have and you take for granted. For example: your family, your friends, your students.

2. Before you fall asleep at night, be thankful for one thing that brought you happiness and joy today.

Reference to p. 6
Daily One Minute Meditation

DAY 10

PRACTICE POSITIVE AFFIRMATIONS

Positive affirmations can be very powerful tools to help you transform your life, while imprinting positivity in your subconscious mind. An affirmation repeated over and over again has the ability to open your mind to accepting the concept.

On the level of Awareness, you focused on discovering yourself, using different tools and techniques. These tools help you explore who you are and discover the teacher within you. Affirmations can bring value in the process of this discovery, helping you to become calm and peaceful in the present moment. They create a mindset of positive thinking, lowering your negative thoughts and becoming aware of your words. It becomes easier for you to practice love and kindness with yourself and your students and to become grateful for the things you have. This can open a door to new opportunities in your life. When you start your day on a positive tone, you find the energy to stay focused on solutions, rather than on complaints, even when things don't go the way you hoped. Positive affirmations can remind you of those things you believe in but sometimes forget because you get distracted by overwhelming thoughts. Ingrain them in your memory for the times when you need them most.

As teachers, we often encourage our students to practice a growth mindset, not to accept phrases like: "I can't do this," or "I will never succeed." Positive affirmations can help you and your students reprogram your minds and look into the world of possibilities instead of a world where nothing is possible. This will boost their confidence and bring motivation to their learning.

DAILY PRACTICE

Focus on the positive affirmations below. Read them slowly and think about what they mean to you. Choose one and make it your own.

I choose positive thoughts from the moment I wake up.

Positive thinking is a natural part of who I am.

I accept and embrace my experiences.

I teach with love and kindness.

I am grateful to be a teacher.

Reference to p. 6
Daily One Minute Meditation

Notes

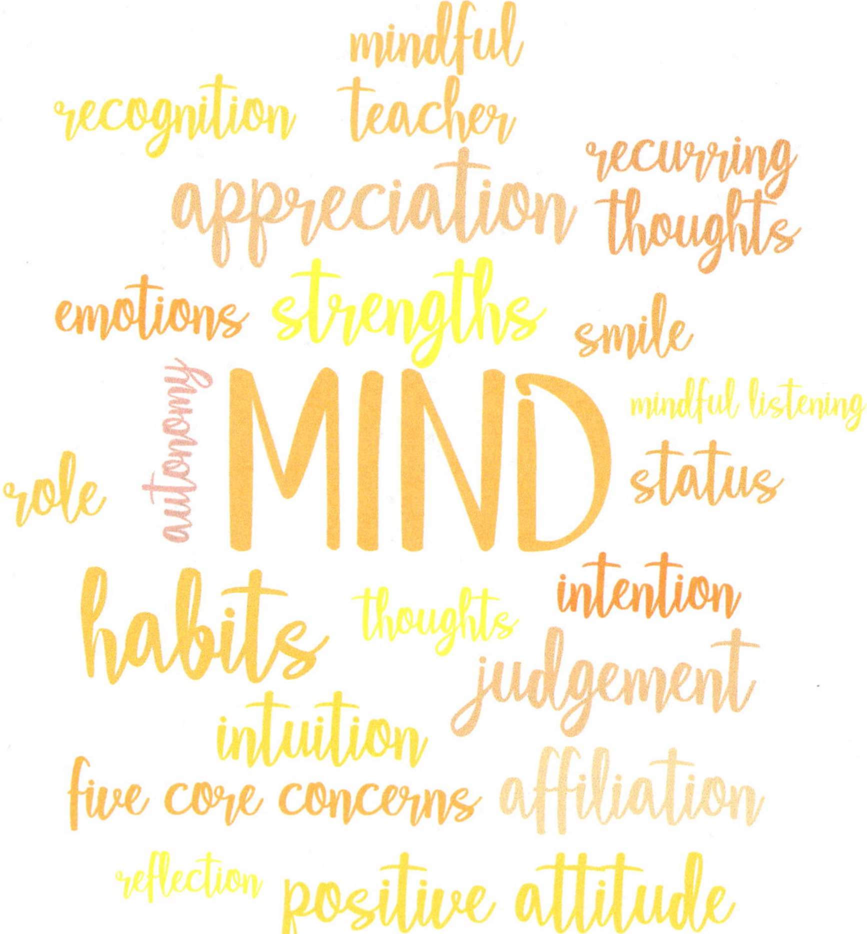
mindful
recognition
teacher
recurring thoughts
appreciation
emotions
strengths
smile
autonomy
MIND
mindful listening
role
status
habits
thoughts
intention
judgement
intuition
five core concerns
affiliation
reflection
positive attitude

LEVEL TWO

RECOGNITION

recognition

CHAPTER TWO

RECOGNIZE YOUR THOUGHTS

Recognition, Level Two, is your journey of self-analysis. Everything starts with the awareness of your thoughts and words, and with the results of your actions.

Many of your thoughts exist without you acknowledging them. In time, they may overwhelm you, creating anxiety and stress. When you start listening to your inner voice, you will make a difference between positive thoughts that help you go forward and negative thoughts that don't serve your needs but drain your power and energy.

As you continue to become aware of your thoughts, you discover more and more about yourself. You learn that you can release your stress by releasing negative and recurrent thoughts, as well as unwanted habits. A positive attitude gives you the power to change old thinking patterns and bring joy and gratitude in your life.

In Chapter Two, you will continue the journey for the next ten days with actions to raise the awareness of your thinking pattern.

Day 11. Be Aware of Your Thoughts

Day 12. Recognize Recurring Thoughts

Day 13. Know the Difference Between Positive and Negative Stress

Day 14. Recognize and Replace Your Unwanted Habits

Day 15. Turn on the Light of Positive Attitude

Day 16. Choose the Power to Change

Day 17. Avoid Judgmental Thoughts

Day 18. Be Aware of Your Intuition

Day 19. Set Your Intentions

Day 20. Feedback

DAY 11

BE AWARE OF YOUR THOUGHTS

You are bound to think thoughts. Your thoughts are words and sentences in your mind, wandering all the time, and you cannot stop thinking them just as you cannot stop the clouds floating in the sky. Thoughts are an integral part of your life and you may have the feeling they control your every action; however, they don't necessarily have to do so.

Sometimes, we confuse our thoughts with our reality. A thought will only become real if you give it full attention and bring it to life. The thought is within you and it appears only for you; you can only imagine it, but you can't actually see it, touch it or smell it. It is not real until you become aware of it and act upon it. Your thoughts don't exist outside of your awareness. When you come to this realization, you will no longer be attached to them and release those thoughts that don't do you any good. You need to become aware of your thoughts, so you have the power to decide how you want to act on them.

Bruce, a high school French language teacher said, "My thoughts came rushing into my head. I decided to write them down so they don't haunt me all day long. This is what my list looked like: 'I forgot to pick up the order at the *pharmacy. My mother needs milk. I have to finish the lesson for tomorrow. Kids weren't responsive and it was my fault. The staff meeting was too long yesterday. I have to return Susie's book to the library. I forgot to take dinner out of the freezer.' I couldn't stop these thoughts. I just realized I was in an endless loop."*

Bruce was overwhelmed by the multitude of thoughts in his mind. He realized he couldn't go on like that. When he decided to write down his thoughts, they swirled around in his mind. Once he saw them on paper, he became aware of what was going on in his mind and prioritized them, giving full attention to the meaningful ones.

All day long, you may have various thoughts, just like Bruce. You too may feel like you are drowning in a deluge of thoughts about the things you must do. These thoughts are going to appear; they cannot be avoided. However, when there are too many and you cannot handle them anymore, take a break for a few seconds to process the information. Write down your thoughts so you can get a new perspective of how they come and go, and how much pressure they put on your mind. When you become aware of them, you become aware of your feelings too. A few deep breaths can also make a big difference.

DAILY PRACTICE

Place a notepad and pen next to you. Take between 5-10 minutes today to write down your thoughts. Be aware of as many thoughts as you can. Stop when your time is up and read those thoughts. Don't judge them, just see if you can prioritize them. You will feel less stress when you realize you have some control over them.

ONE MINUTE MEDITATION FOR CHAPTER 2

Find a comfortable seated position.

Close your eyes or lower your gaze.

Rest your hands in your lap, palms up.

Inhale through your nose for 4 counts.

Exhale through your mouth for 6 counts.

Bring your awareness to your breath.

Notice that your mind wanders.

Name each thought:

"Friend" "Anxiety" "Memory" "Future"

Say to yourself, "I accept my thoughts"

Then let them float off like balloons.

Come back to your breath.

Inhale through your nose for 4 counts.

Exhale through your mouth for 6 counts.

Recognize your choice to remain in the *here* and *now*.

Smile as you slowly open your eyes!

DAY 12

RECOGNIZE RECURRING THOUGHTS

Your thoughts guide your emotions and feelings. Don't despair if you have negative thoughts, everyone has them. But they don't have to overtake your life. Negative thoughts have strong roots in your mind because it is hard to convince yourself that the thought is wrong. When you realize you don't want to think about it, you actually end up thinking more about it, while trying hard not to. As a teacher, you might not realize how recurrent thoughts influence your teaching. Try not to think about the students who are disruptive in your class and you will find yourself thinking only about them, to the detriment of others. Those negative thoughts do not serve you. Try relaxing your body and don't judge your thoughts.

Think about the two teachers described in the narrative below. Do you identify with either one? They choose different thoughts. While one brings on positive emotions through her thoughts, the other does not.

Meet teacher colleagues Ron and Liz, both physical education teachers in the same school. Ron is getting a divorce and is angry most of the time. *"I feel my ex-wife is ungrateful for all I have done, and she says I have a negative outlook on life. She has no idea how the stress affects me physically and in my daily work, and how hard it is for me to keep up with my students' needs."* Liz works hard on her relationship with her spouse. She recently had health problems and is trying to build her strength. She recognizes the need to lower her stress levels. *"I feel the daily stress would take up all my energy. However, I know I have to stay calm for my own well-being, if I want to recover soon. When I feel any kind of stress, I give myself permission to feel sad at times, and then I focus on what*

I have and what I can be grateful for. I say out loud, 'Okay, Liz, time's up. Let's look at the sunshine and be thankful for this moment.'"

Both Ron and Liz deal with stress. But while Ron doesn't recognize he can control his thoughts, Liz does.

Once you have recognized your negative thoughts, recognize the physical symptoms of your stress. Then, you can stop the recurrent thoughts from taking away your energy and instead focus on your achievements or solutions to your negative thoughts. Mindful relaxation can help you reduce this stress. It can be a gateway to refresh your mind from attention fatigue and increase your awareness of the present moment.

Back to Liz. She gained manifold benefits from her daily mindful relaxation exercises. Here's how she describes her experience:

"When I enter a state of mindful relaxation, I get physical and mental benefits. I can actually lower my blood pressure and heart rate. Additionally, my breathing becomes more stable. This helps me control my fear and allows me to live in the moment and enjoy my life."

DAILY PRACTICE

When your mind is trapped in recurrent thoughts, you unconsciously go back to those thoughts over and over again. One way to release the pressure of these thoughts is to focus on your breath and bring your attention back to the present moment.

Find a comfortable place and sit with your body straight and still. Focus on your breath. Be aware of your breath as you inhale and exhale. Take three breaths and focus on these questions:

- Is your breath warm or cold?
- Is your inhaled breath long or short?
- Is your exhaled breath the same length?
- Do you notice a short pause between the inhaled and exhaled breaths?

Make your inhaled and exhaled breaths last the same amount of time.

Continue to tune into your breath as you breathe in and breathe out for 4-6 times.

You will think thoughts; this is normal. If your mind wanders, calmly and without judgment, bring your thoughts back to your breath.

Continue to breathe normally now and feel the relaxation extend throughout your body. Reflect on how you feel when you have completed this exercise.

Reference to p. 38
Daily One Minute Meditation

DAY 13

KNOW THE DIFFERENCE BETWEEN POSITIVE AND NEGATIVE STRESS

Stress is not necessarily connected to negative experiences. We may think it is caused by circumstances beyond our control that generate negative stress. However, it's not only the external demand that causes stress, it's also connected to your perceptions.

Positive stress gives you the opportunity to go on and progress in different situations, such as working on a new project, preparing for a show or an event, etc. Positive stress usually lasts for a short time, and it most often occurs in exceptional situations. It can inspire you and help you grow and become a better person.

Negative stress, on the other hand, is based on patterns of negative thoughts; they drain your energy. They can last for long periods of time (days, weeks, even years) and can become chronic. Negative stress can make you worry about the future, bringing on depression or even despair.

Let's look at the stress you experience during a typical school day. It can come from too many papers to grade, challenging students, a project with a close deadline, an argument with a colleague, and so on. When the stress is negative, everything about you changes. Your gestures change, your posture and your tone of voice change, your body language and even the way you walk and talk can change.

Recognize how your body responds to these negative thoughts. Is your body tight? Do your shoulders become stiff or slump? Does your face clench? What about your jaw? Do your hands become cold or hot? Ask yourself, "What makes my body react this way? Is this stress good for me or not?"

When you are aware of your negative stress, you have the choice to release it. Instead of being drained by it, bring your attention back to the present moment and focus on the positive aspects of life. This brings the stress from a negative perspective to a positive one and motivates you to achieve your goals and strengthen your self-esteem.

Remember that your students also face similar challenges. Talk to them about the difference they can make in their lives when they focus on the positive aspects of stress. When you teach them, they gain and so do you. You are reinforcing these concepts within yourself.

DAILY PRACTICE

Since stress has a direct effect on your body, this next "walking" practice connected to your senses can help release the tension inside you and help you become aware of the present moment. It will give you the chance to consciously choose to reduce your stress.

Take a deep breath as you begin your walk.

Feel the sole of your foot touching the ground.

Notice things around you.

Focus on them as you walk for about one minute.

After the first minute, add sounds and smells. What do you hear? What do you smell?

Now add something you can touch. It can be a piece of clothing or just a pebble, if you are outdoors.

At this point, you are focused on four senses; they reconnect you with your surroundings: sight, sound, smell, and touch. They give you a sense of self-awareness and release the stress you feel in your body.

Reference to p. 38
Daily One Minute Meditation

DAY 14

RECOGNIZE AND REPLACE YOUR UNWANTED HABITS

Awareness of your thoughts leads to awareness of your actions and, eventually, awareness of your habits. Through the years you have developed all kinds of habits. Healthy habits are the ones that contribute to the accomplishment of your daily tasks, giving you energy to go on. Unwanted habits create negative stress, consume your time, and prevent you from achieving your goals.

Unwanted habits are based on actions taken in the past and supported by routines. They often address a certain need you might not even recognize. When you become aware of the need and the habit associated to it, you can choose to replace it with a healthy behavior that addresses that same need. For example, if you eat sweets under stress, choose to replace them with vegetables. Gain awareness of your needs and the associated habits and their health benefits. If you are not aware of them, they will drive you on auto-pilot, causing health problems and building up negative stress.

If you become mindful when you use your bad habits, you will not let them anchor you in the fears of the past or in the worries of the future. You will be able to live in the present moment and replace the unwanted habits with ones that serve you.

As we all know, unhealthy habits can manifest as addictions, anxiety, self-sabotage, and blame. When you are drawn into a negative habit, ask yourself, *"What are my thoughts right now? What need triggered this behavior? How many times do I do it each day?"* Once you recognize your thoughts, you gain the power to change them.

Fred, a high school math teacher, spent about four hours a day on social media. As a result, he would not get a full night rest and would, therefore, end up going to school unprepared. He knew his addiction was adversely impacting his teaching; sometimes, he could not even concentrate during class.

Fred said, *"At times, I would forget what I had already told my students. This would be so stressful that I would become angry at my students because they weren't paying attention! But it wasn't their fault. It was mine."*

Fred had unwanted habits leading to negative stress. He became short tempered during school hours because he was not getting enough sleep at night. He would always end up with headaches and stress. When he realized that his behavior was triggered by the need to be connected with others, he reflected on his thoughts and opened his mind to other possibilities to fulfill this need. He decided to spend his time socializing with his friends and colleagues instead of spending time online.

Breathing awareness, and meditation helped Fred change his habits in order to meet his needs. He shared his story with his students and asked them to name an unwanted habit, identify the need that triggered it, and then choose to replace it.

DAILY PRACTICE

Make a list of all your habits – both healthy and unwanted. Choose one and reflect upon it. You can learn more about yourself by looking at either a positive or a negative habit.

Reflect on the following questions.

1. What are my thoughts about this habit?

2. What need triggered this habit?

3. Is it a healthy or an unwanted habit? (cravings, addictions, etc.)

4. Does it keep me away from enjoying the present moment? (excessive TV, technology, etc.)

5. Does it add stress to my life? (smoking, drinking, negative thinking, etc.)

6. What did I learn from examining this habit? If it is an unwanted one, how can I replace it?

Reference to p. 38
Daily One Minute Meditation

DAY 15

TURN ON THE LIGHT OF POSITIVE ATTITUDE

Your thoughts and attitude reflect the way you live your life. Throughout this chapter, we have discussed awareness of your thoughts and the influence they have on your stress levels. Let's now look at the way your attitude can influence you. When you feel that nothing works and your energy is low, become aware of your attitude and adjust it so that you think positively. This helps you find solutions and overcome difficult situations.

When you wander in darkness, trying to find solutions, you feel drained of energy, unable to see your way out, often thinking negative thoughts. Those thoughts are often exaggerated and not completely true: *"I can't see the solutions. Nothing ever works for me."* Nothing ever works for you? Surely that doesn't happen. Sometimes something does!

Instead, imagine your positive attitude is a flashlight that lights your way in the dark, helping you find your path and the solutions you've been searching for. You turn on the flashlight and see what's inside you. Your attitude comes from inside you, and, when you decide to turn it on, you see things clearly and become aware of what feels right. Your positive thinking is energizing, and you become proactive rather than reactive. It takes courage and commitment to turn the flashlight on and get rid of your worries and fears. But when you do, the light illuminates your mood. Your positive thoughts and strengths are aligned, and you accomplish your goals and overcome your obstacles.

Turn on the light of positive attitude

Maria is an English teacher, passionate and enthusiastic, teaching each class with the ultimate intention of bringing the joy of learning into the classroom. She shared her story with us:

"*After the first term of the school year, I was asked to replace a colleague and take over his class for the rest of the year. When I entered this class for the first time, I felt rejection and judgment; everything I said or did was questioned by my students, doubt reflecting in their eyes. Over the following weeks, they kept sending me negative feedback through their attitude. I couldn't stop thinking that this was the class with the most difficult students ever. After a while, it became hard for me to even enter this classroom; I was angry and frustrated. I knew I had to do something to change this situation. I started to reflect on my own attitude to understand when and how my teaching went wrong. I thought about my strengths and the first thing that came to my mind was my creativity. One thing I knew for sure: I was creative and I wanted to make learning enjoyable. The idea struck me instantly: creative writing! The next time I entered the classroom, I took along notebooks and colored pencils for each student and invited them to think about writing a book that could become a future best seller. I told them to create a title for this book, and I wanted the content to be about having a positive attitude. Debates and discussions followed. My students accepted this challenge; they realized how easy it was to get trapped in an atmosphere of negativity and how positive attitude can be a driver for change. They even imagined their books stacked on a shelf labeled "Positive Attitude."*"

The students were far more creative than Maria could have imagined. The lesson Maria learned from this experience was that positive attitude helps overcome challenges and improves teaching. She understood that being flexible and open minded made for better communication with her students.

DAILY PRACTICE

Take a look at Maria's situation. She didn't look at the rejection she received from her students, rather at the opportunity for them to create something new. Next time, when you find yourself in a difficult situation, reflect on the following questions: *"What lesson can I learn from this situation?" "How can I overcome this challenge?"* Turn on the light of positive attitude!

Reference to p. 38
Daily One Minute Meditation

DAY 16

CHOOSE THE POWER TO CHANGE

If you want to make the world a better place, take a look at yourself and make a change! – Michael Jordan

When we speak about change, we don't necessarily have to think about changing who we are or the way we live our life. The need for change doesn't mean that what we do is wrong. However, in life, there is always room for improvement and improvement brings change. There are times when you have to give up on something in order to build something new. Focus on the idea that things can become better and don't label them "wrong."

Maria's lesson about attitude taught us about the power within to change. She managed to bring back creativity and enthusiasm into her teaching only when she chose to give up her negative feelings of anger and frustration.

Everything starts with the awareness of your thoughts and words and ends with the actions you are committed to take. As we already know, thoughts become words and words become actions. The words you use may create stress and raise anxiety. However, a new thinking pattern will change the way you connect and relate to others. If you eliminate stress-related words, you can bring gratitude and joy to your life.

Instead of "I have to go to school every day," say "I enjoy going to school every day." This way, you transform an obligation ("have to") into an action, creating a positive mindset. Your words make a big difference in your attitude. Embrace positive thoughts and words so that you may embrace a positive attitude. It doesn't mean negative thoughts and words won't exist, but you will decide what your focus will be. It becomes your choice.

Make one small change a day to lower your stress and make room for happiness and joy to enter your life. One change at a time can create a chain of changes in your life.

DAILY PRACTICE

Your breath is connected with your thoughts, emotions, and feelings. Imagine a situation when you were upset or angry. Think of your breath at that time and remember how it made you feel.

Now, imagine that you can go back to the same situation, but, this time, you can change your breathing pattern, focusing on the way you inhale and exhale deeply. How do you feel this time?

When you become aware of your thoughts, words or actions, you can choose to change what doesn't serve you. Small changes, like correcting the way you breathe, can bring you peace and awareness. Small changes can make big differences.

Reference to p. 38
Daily One Minute Meditation

DAY 17

AVOID JUDGMENTAL THOUGHTS

Through the process of gaining awareness and recognizing your thoughts, you may encounter judgmental thoughts that undermine your self-esteem, limiting your development and growth. This limitation begins with the labels you put consciously or unconsciously on yourself. Like most people, you too may be addicted to labeling things into good or bad, separating them through the labels you assigned them. You may find yourself using labels such as, "I'm a perfectionist," or "I'm always late," "I'm a fast eater," "I'm chaotic," "I'm unhappy." When you label yourself, you tend to accept these categories and make them your beliefs and truths. You do not take responsibility for your actions, instead you blame the label.

If you gain awareness of your thoughts, you can recognize the labels you use and realize they don't define who you are. Listen to your thoughts and nail them down, don't let them nail you down.

Let's imagine the old Cherokee Indian story of the two wolves, constantly fighting each other. The story says: *We all have two wolves inside us. They are in our mind, constantly fighting each other. There is a white wolf and a dark grey wolf. The dark grey wolf is filled with fear, anger, envy, and arrogance. The white wolf is filled with love, hope, courage, and compassion. Which will be the winner? The one that you feed.*

If we reflect on Maria's story, about how her students' attitude affected her way of thinking judgmental thoughts, we will realize that she chose to feed her dark grey wolf, empowering her anger and frustration. She also labeled the class as the "most difficult students ever." When she chose to "feed" her mind with positive thoughts, she gained power as the white wolf; she brought hope and courage into her way of thinking and found the strength to go on and accomplish her goal. Once you become aware of the way you think and the labels you use, you will gain the power to overcome the negativity in your life.

DAILY PRACTICE

Reflect on the negative labels you put on yourself and on the way they affect the achievement of your goals. Now pick the one you use most often and imagine that you write it on a blackboard. Look at your imaginary board and slowly wipe off the label.

Focus on your breath for one minute and feel the pressure of the label releasing from your body.

Reflect on how you feel about letting go of the negative thoughts connected to your label.

You may do this practice every time you find judgmental thoughts in your mind and find yourself putting labels on yourself or others.

Reference to p. 38
Daily One Minute Meditation

DAY 18

BE AWARE OF YOUR INTUITION!

Ever since you were born, you have been making choices. Every day, your mind deals with hundreds of these choices. You may be aware of them as they run through your mind on a conscious level. But others work on an unconscious level. The unconscious level recognizes an enormous amount of information that the conscious mind cannot fathom. The challenge is to listen to your inner voice and prevent the conscious mind from drowning it out.

Intuition is that voice you often hear in your head and helps you to make decisions. You intuitively know what feels right or wrong. It's the "aha moment" that looks like a spark in the dark.

Intuition can activate your senses, such as goosebumps on your arms or butterflies in your stomach. Intuition makes the connection with your senses through your deeper feelings. These responses give you confirmation and empower your decisions. You may remember hearing the voice of intuition in your mind saying: *"I felt this, deep down inside me."* If we think back to Maria's story, when she decided to bring her students notebooks so they could write their stories about attitude, her intuition told her this was going to work, and it would help her connect with her students.

When Maria became self-aware and true to herself, it was easier for her to follow her intuition. She brought creativity into the classroom and made learning enjoyable. Her attitude and her students' attitude improved. She followed her intuition and knew what was right for her.

Intuition is recognizing what you inherently know. Some people think of intuition as something mystical and not real. But scientists say it can be identified in lab experiments and visualized on brain scans. Your instincts tell you what you need to do before your conscious thoughts occur. Meditation can help process this intuition. You become aware of things inside you that feel right for you.

DAILY PRACTICE

Consider a decision you need to make. Formulate a question about it before you fall asleep and direct your mind to find an answer overnight. When you wake up, before you even get out of bed, notice what comes first into your mind. This is your intuition kicking in. Go for the answer. You can then decide if you want to follow your intuition!

Reference to p. 38
Daily One Minute Meditation

DAY 19

SET YOUR INTENTIONS

When you are aware of your thinking pattern, you hear your intuition and see the labels you put on yourself. Once that occurs, it's time to create intentions to achieve your goals. Intentions are conscious actions you plan to take with commitment and determination. An intention will successfully materialize when it is followed by a committed plan and determined action. It is best for the intention to have a specific time associated with it.

Here's an example of an intention. You drive your car to school with the intention of getting there by 8 AM. Even if you choose to take a different route to school, you know you are headed there and you know the approximate time you will arrive. You plan to get there on time; this is your intention.

When you have a positive intention, it's easy to apply positive thinking and make your intent a reality. When you have both a positive intention and a positive mindset, your chances to achieve your goals increase dramatically. Positive intentions can be particularly helpful when you have negative thoughts you want to change, but you don't seem to have the motivation to carry out the change. Just like seeds need water and attention in order to grow, intentions need commitment and determination to be realized.

In Maria's case, her intention was to bring the joy of learning into the classroom. She knew this was extremely important to her. Her intention empowered her to persevere when she encountered hardships and gave her the determination to fight her way through to a successful outcome. She relied on her strengths, she had the courage to change, and she found a way to make her classes enjoyable.

DAILY PRACTICE

Set an intention for the day. Define it clearly in your mind and then write it on a piece of paper. Think about how your intention will impact you or others. Include a commitment and your determination.

Set up weekly, monthly or yearly intentions. It is helpful to write them down as a to-do list and take time to check on them regularly.

Look at the intentions below. Which ones would you consider following?

- I will show kindness in my classroom.
- I will model mindful behavior to my students.
- I will listen carefully when my students speak to me.
- I will do a breathing practice daily.
- I will make a student smile every day.

Reference to p. 38
Daily One Minute Meditation

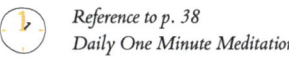

DAY 20

FEEDBACK

Feedback is information about a person, a performance, or an action. When you look beyond the information, you realize that feedback is strongly connected to thoughts and emotions. When you give or receive feedback, it can increase your pulse, your blood pressure, creating stress in your whole body.

Teachers give feedback all the time. It is an essential part of education, helping students raise their awareness about areas of improvement and acknowledge their strengths. Feedback can increase or decrease motivation. Positive feedback is the easiest to take and it motivates you. Negative feedback is not always discouraging if you are prepared to learn from your mistakes and open up to change. If your mind is open and flexible, you will not take feedback as a personal threat, but as an opportunity for personal growth. You want your students to understand the importance of feedback.

As a teacher, you often receive feedback from your students, even when it is not spoken in words; it is reflected by their actions and attitude. In Maria's story, the negative feedback she received from her students angered her and she lost motivation to teach them. However, when she changed her attitude and looked at the feedback as a possibility to grow, she regained her strength and brought creativity back into her teaching. This challenged the entire class and they all gained from her resourcefulness.

Feedback helps you and your students set goals and develop commitments. The feedback should be kind, helpful, and specific. This way, it can increase motivation and develop a relation based on respect and responsibility.

Be aware of your timing when you give feedback. The right moment maximizes its effect and impact whether the feedback is going to a colleague or to your students. Be sensitive to others and think of how they may react to what you are about to say.

DAILY PRACTICE

When you are aware of your emotions and feelings, you can also become aware of your students' emotions and feelings.

When you give feedback to your students, breathing exercises can help you become calm, empathic, and compassionate.

You may practice this breathing exercise three to four times.

Inhale while counting to 4

Exhale while counting to 6

You will smile when you finish this exercise

Reference to p. 38
Daily One Minute Meditation

CHAPTER THREE

RECOGNIZE YOUR EMOTIONS

Chapter Two guided you on your path towards the awareness and recognition of your thoughts. Your journey to discover your *Teacher Within* will continue in this chapter, while exploring your emotions and the ways they affect your mind and body.

We all have emotions that can either add to our lives and make us happy, or detract from our lives and cause us stress. In this chapter, you will explore the Five Core Concerns that will motivate you and generate helpful emotions for you and your students. You will discover an easy-to-use framework to help you in the classroom when emotions rise, and when you find yourself struggling to effectively deal with them. You will always have emotions. To feel and understand them can help you live a happier life. To know how to use them effectively can give you more meaning.

Appreciation, affiliation, autonomy, status, and role are the Five Core Concerns, important to almost all of us. You can turn your attention to these core concerns to address the emotions you feel and then tailor your actions toward a positive outcome. With knowledge about these concerns, you will be able to gauge the needs of your students, set the emotional tone in the classroom, and create a mutually acceptable learning environment for you and your students. This practical and straightforward advice is based on the book *Beyond Reason: Using Emotions as You Negotiate,* by Roger Fisher and Daniel Shapiro.

To become a good manager of your emotions, we suggest you deeply reflect through the following over the next ten days:

Day 21. Be Aware of Your Emotions
Day 22. The Story of the Five Core Concerns
Day 23. Express Appreciation
Day 24. Build Affiliation
Day 25. Respect Autonomy
Day 26. Acknowledge Status
Day 27. Understand Your Roles
Day 28. Take Initiative: Address the Concern
Day 29. Embrace the Five Core Concerns
Day 30. Practice Affirmations

DAY 21

BE AWARE OF YOUR EMOTIONS!

You create your thoughts and they lead you to the emotions you experience. Emotions can be wonderful, helpful and also challenging. Think of your students. Each student has his or her own thoughts and emotions. And so do you.

An emotion can be explained as a felt experience. You feel an emotion; it follows your thought. When someone says or does something significant to you, your emotions respond, along with your thoughts. And just as thoughts, emotions can be positive or negative. When you are uplifted, you are experiencing a positive emotion. Negative emotions, on the other hand, can cause stress, anger, and/or frustration.

Here are three indisputable truths: You have emotions. You cannot stop having them. You cannot ignore them. These three facts of life will show that emotions can have a positive or negative impact in your classroom. They can impair the standard and efficacy of your teaching and, in some cases, could create havoc in the classroom. But they don't have to...

If you learn to recognize your emotions and find ways to directly deal with them, you will overcome your challenges. Positive emotions reduce fear and suspicion, so your students will feel safe in the classroom. Positive emotions will also motivate you and your students. Things get done more efficiently as you and your students work together with increased emotional commitment. Your students are more open to listen to you and you enhance their learning experience.

For the next nine days, you will understand how to use the "Five Core Concerns" framework to address the emotions you face in the classroom. The five core concerns will be your ready-to-use tools for dealing with your emotions. You will learn to define and become aware of your role, status, autonomy, affiliation, and need for appreciation. As you follow through with your daily reading, think about how these five core concerns stimulate positive emotions for you and for your students.

The five core concerns are not completely distinct from one another. So, it is important to realize that they blend, mix, and merge. Each one contributes to the whole. When you use these Core Concerns, you will stimulate positive emotions and will treat your students with fairness, honesty, and consistency.

DAILY PRACTICE

Think about a difficult situation you have recently experienced with one of your students and you felt strong negative emotions. Recall some of your emotions and think of the way you reacted at that moment. Don't blame your student. Were you overwhelmed? Were you fair to yourself and to your student?

Daily One Minute Meditation

ONE MINUTE MEDITATION FOR CHAPTER 3

Find a comfortable seated position.
Close your eyes or lower your gaze.
Rest your hands in your lap, palms up.
Allow your mind to be clear and present.
Bring your awareness to your breath.
Inhale through your nose for 4 counts.
Exhale through your mouth for 6 counts.
Take your hand to your heart.
Notice your heartbeat.
Think about a moment in your day that frustrated you.
Notice any changes in your heartbeat.
Think of a moment that excited you.
Notice any changes in your heartbeat.
Release those moments.
Come back to your breath.
Inhale through your nose for 4 counts.
Exhale through your mouth for 6 counts
Be aware of your body's emotional responses.
Acknowledge them and let them go.
Smile as you slowly open your eyes!

DAY 22

THE STORY OF THE FIVE CORE CONCERNS

Mr. Appreciation and Ms. Status are both teachers. He works in the elementary school and she teaches high school students. They met at the first staff meeting of the year, when Mr. Appreciation, the new teacher in this school, walked into the staff room and smiled at Ms. Status. However,. she turned her head and focused on marking her papers. Annoyed, he did not feel welcome. Then, Ms. Affiliation, an elementary school teacher, strolled into the room followed by a rigid faced Dr. Principal Role. To Mr. Appreciation, none of them seemed friendly. Dr. Principal Role was about to start the meeting, when Mrs. Autonomy stormed into the room and said, *"Let's begin with introductions. New teachers, please stand."* Meanwhile, Dr. Principal Role looked at her wondering why she was taking over his staff meeting.

The staff meeting ended, and the teachers went to their classrooms. Mr. Appreciation was not satisfied. He couldn't figure out the teacher's role during the staff meeting. He tried to let his feelings go. He greeted his students but felt unsettled. As the day progressed, the students bore the brunt of his frustrations. *"Let's begin. Each student, please stand up, tell us your name and one thing about yourself."* The day dragged on and he just couldn't regroup.

At lunch, Ms. Affiliation walked into his classroom. *"How are you? I would like to share with you a bit about my experience in this school."* Mr. Appreciation took a deep breath and smiled. Finally, someone was kind. After school, the two of them walked to their cars. Ms. Status hurried up to them and said, *"I was expecting a different welcome after the summer break. Last year, all my students passed their exams with As and Bs! An amazing achievement! I am so frustrated, nobody said anything to me! Besides, most of my colleagues knew I had surgery this summer and no one seemed to care how I was doing either! What's going on?"* Tension built as they said goodbye. Mr. Appreciation got in his car and thought about his high expectations before the morning meeting.

When he arrived home, Mr. Appreciation told his wife, *"I don't need medals of appreciation for being there, but the morning staff meeting ruined my day. Thank goodness this teacher, Ms. Affiliation, came into my classroom with a positive attitude, and we ended up talking about our families. Tomorrow will be a better day."*

DAILY PRACTICE

Recall your first day of school this year.

What thoughts and emotions did you have? Did you connect with your fellow teachers? If you did, how? If you didn't, why?

Reflect on these questions and on your answers. What would you have done differently?

Reference to p. 66
Daily One Minute Meditation

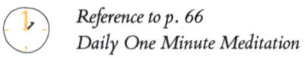

DAY 23

EXPRESS APPRECIATION

The story you read yesterday was based on the difficult behavior patterns and emotions the staff experienced. Think back to Mr. Appreciation and how he felt when he wasn't appreciated by the staff. He couldn't get over it for the rest of the day. It either feels really good when you are appreciated, or it feels really awful when you aren't. When you feel appreciated, you feel valued, and when you don't feel appreciated, you may feel rejected or ignored.

Each character was dealing with challenging emotions but, through the five core concerns, we can examine his/her emotional state and how best he/she could take appropriate action. We will explore these emotions for the next several days, so you can begin to use this concept in the classroom.

We start with the first core concern, appreciation. Appreciation is sensitive awareness and recognition of the good qualities of a person, including yourself, embracing the individual's unique personality. Appreciation is one of the most important core values. To understand how appreciation works, let's think about it from two different perspectives.

PERSPECTIVE 1:

You say to your students, *"You will have to do at least one hour of homework every day, or you won't pass my class."*

Several students look at you angrily and you end up feeling frustrated. Your intention is to help them complete their work and make progress. You want them to hear and understand your point of view.

"This is for your own good," you say.

You want them not only to understand your point of view but also to see its value. But they don't get it.

You say, *"This isn't for me. It's for you."* And it still doesn't work. So, what's going on?

These firm requirements are actually about your need to be appreciated by your students. Even if your intentions are well-meaning and you want them to learn from doing their homework, you are looking through the lens of negative emotions in this case. This, in turn, makes your own attitude negative.

PERSPECTIVE 2:

Here is a different way to approach the same situation.

"I wonder how we can figure out a way for you to get your work done. Are there any suggestions?"

One of your students, Meg, says, *"I feel frustrated. I've tried to understand the material and now I'm afraid I won't pass even if I spend time on it. I don't get it."*

And you answer, *"You must be frustrated, Meg. Is anybody else feeling the same?"*

Several hands go up.

You say, *"Let's go over the concepts so you understand them clearly. If you don't understand me, raise your hand, and I will go over them again.*

You still have to do one hour of homework every day, but I appreciate your input, Meg."

You found merit in what Meg said, and you acknowledged it. You didn't say you didn't expect her to do the work. You told her she still had to do one hour of homework every day. The class started to respond with more positive energy and, this way, you got involved in their thought process. Finally, with a positive attitude, Meg did understand the material!

In the second scenario, you looked at the situation through a lens of positive emotions. You found merit and your attitude toward your students became positive as well.

In most cases, you do not benefit from trying to argue your perspective. Instead, try to understand the students' perspective. Don't listen for the weaknesses in their argument. Instead, keep an ear out for something you can understand and can move in a positive direction.

To show appreciation to your students, consider the following suggestions:

- Understand their point of view. Listen carefully to what they are saying. Watch their body language. Find a way to communicate that you have heard, seen, and understood them.

- Find merit in what they think, feel, or do by using statements such as *"Congrats! I'm really proud of your work!"*

- Share your understanding with kind words, actions, and compassion. This does not mean you are giving in to their will. You are learning to appreciate their point of view.

DAILY PRACTICE

Think of a situation when a colleague or a student was disrespectful. Use the following questions to guide you. As you read them, recognize your thoughts and become aware of your feelings.

What were your thoughts at the time? How did you feel?

What is the negative feeling you remember?

Do you think the other person may have misunderstood you?

What could you have done to inspire appreciation?

Reference to p. 66
Daily One Minute Meditation

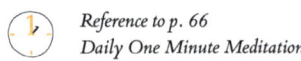

DAY 24

BUILD AFFILIATION

Recognize the links or connections you have with someone with whom you interact daily. These connections can be related to your job, age, common interests, favorite books, or you may think of any other connection. Pay attention to how you have developed this connection and why it is meaningful to you.

Affiliation, the second Core Concern, means bonding or connecting. If you have a good connection with another person, you are more likely to share a good relationship. Positive emotions can build trust and affiliation. There are numerous ways to develop affiliation. Once again, think about the staff meeting and Mr. Appreciation, who didn't feel appreciated, and about Ms. Status, who needed affiliation desperately.

Mr. Appreciation could have taken the initiative. When Ms. Autonomy asked them to stand up and introduce themselves, he could have taken a leap of faith and said, *"It's my first day in school! I'll reach out to all of you to help me start off on the right foot!"* With a smile, he would have then sat down. In this case, Mr. Appreciation would be trying to connect with the teachers.

While he might need to work hard to establish a connection with the teachers in the new school, Mr. Appreciation could also have asked questions and shown the teachers his willingness to connect. He'll need to recognize when the time is appropriate for a chat, and he'll also understand there are situations when people may not feel comfortable discussing their lives. Ms. Status was open about her health issue and her feelings of rejection, but other teachers might not have been. Mr. Appreciation could benefit from recognizing such emotions and try to connect with his colleagues.

DAILY PRACTICE

When you are aware of the need to develop close relationships with your fellow teachers, you build long-lasting affiliation. Ask yourself the following questions:

What can I do to consolidate my current relationships and to develop new ones?

How can I develop meaningful working relations with my colleagues?

Close your eyes for two minutes and reflect on your answers.

Today's challenge is to reach out to one of your colleagues to learn more about him/her.

Reference to p. 66
Daily One Minute Meditation

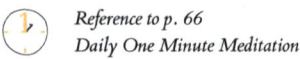

DAY 25

RESPECT AUTONOMY

Autonomy, the third Core Concern, is your freedom to make decisions, without nudging or impositions from a third party. As we have previously discussed, the Five Core Concerns are connected to your emotions. If you make the right decisions and use your autonomy, you will avoid some of those recurrent negative emotions.

When Ms. Autonomy told the teachers to stand up and introduce themselves, she was impinging on the autonomy of Dr. Principal Role. She limited his participation in decision-making. Reflect on Dr. Principal Role's emotions at this point. How often do you feel your autonomy is limited?

How aware are you of the autonomy you have in your life? You know you have autonomy in your classroom. You choose the lessons, decide who sits where, and form the class routine. In fact, you are instrumental in creating the class culture. But what about your students? Recognize you are not alone in deciding how the class environment is created. When you exclude students from this process, you limit their participation in decision-making and impinge on their autonomy. The case of the classroom is no different from the situation at the staff meeting. Who had autonomy in that meeting? How do you think the other teachers felt? As teachers, we should reflect on these two questions more often.

We should also consider our personal life outside the classroom and reflect on our autonomy. In both instances, we make decisions, and we need to consider other people's opinions. When we assume responsibility for our decisions, we will understand to what extent we are comfortable with our own decisions or we would rather prefer that other people will make the decisions for us. Fear of mistakes and failure should not become obstacles in our endeavor to succeed and become role models for our students.

DAILY PRACTICE

Think about a situation when somebody did not respect your autonomy. Be aware of your thoughts and emotions and recognize them. Reflect on your emotions.

How did that situation make you feel?

What you could have done differently to restore your autonomy?

Reference to p. 66
Daily One Minute Meditation

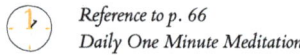

DAY 26

ACKNOWLEDGE STATUS

Status is the fourth Core Concern, and it also deals with your emotions. According to Dictionary.com, status is: *"the position of an individual in relation to others, especially in regard to social or professional standing."* Status can generate positive emotions. Or, it can cause distress, if it's connected to a lack of recognition, as in the case of Ms. Status, one of the top performing teachers in the school, whose students had the best exam results. She felt a lack of status with the other teachers even though she had success with her students. Her need for status was strong, not only because of her role and contribution to her class performance, but also because she had overcome personal challenges while striving for outstanding results.

When you feel your status is undermined, your focus shifts towards negative emotions. You may feel rejected, inferior, angry or any other such negative emotions. The perceived status of those within a group can make some people more visible than others. Those who don't have high visibility may lack confidence and may feel the urge to compete in a bid to remove their perceived invisibility. Ms. Status felt a similar lack of recognition for her status when none of her colleagues acknowledged her presence, remembered her achievements or her serious health issues.

What does status mean for a teacher and how can it be recognized by students and colleagues? Recognizing someone's status is not about the power held by the person who has the final word. As an educator, your status should be about your knowledge, attitude, and character, aligned with the desire to teach and inspire your students. Status, in this case, has more to do with how you feel within yourself than with how you are perceived by others.

Think about the strength of the status you have within yourself. You definitely have a status as a teacher, but do you recognize this deep within yourself? Are you always comfortable with how you perceive it? How do you deal with your emotions when your status is not recognized? Do you feel valued for who you are? If not, how can you change so you feel valued? The path begins within you.

DAILY PRACTICE

Think of a situation in your school when your status was not recognized by your colleagues, your students or by their parents.

What thoughts and emotions dominated your thinking? How did you deal with the situation?

Think of a situation in your classroom when you did not recognize a student's status. What were your thoughts at that time? Was that situation connected to your own status in the classroom?

Share with your students why status is important and what it means to you.

Reference to p. 66
Daily One Minute Meditation

DAY 27

UNDERSTAND YOUR ROLES

Roles can be your purposes in a situation, organization, or relationship. They help define your identity. People may play multiple roles during their lifetime, and these roles change constantly according to circumstance, situation, life-experience, and/or expectations. When you understand your roles, you can have more clarity and consistency in your actions.

Consider your role as a teacher. Are you comfortable in this role? What does it mean to you? What are your other roles and how do you feel about them?

Your role in a situation may be temporary and may not last long, or it may be conventional and last for years. Temporary roles could be those of a listener, partner, orator, problem solver, negotiator, or even a guest or a host. You have the power to choose those roles you like and those you dislike. However, conventional roles are different. Conventional roles are those you play in an organization and within the community. You may have roles as a teacher, nurse, writer, lawyer, doctor, director, manager or scientist, etc. In relationships, your role can be a parent, son/daughter, brother/sister, friend, spouse, and so on.

Whether your role is temporary or conventional, you will want it to have a clear purpose and meaning for you. Additionally, you will want a fulfilling role. Imagine, in the story discussed previously, the many roles of Dr. Principal Role. He is the Principal, the people manager, the role model for the teachers, as well as the advisor in a meeting, the teacher in several classrooms, as well as the husband and father in his family. His roles extend to the classroom and beyond.

Once you have become aware of your roles and you acknowledge them, you will enhance the clarity of your role as a teacher. A fulfilling role has a deep personal meaning for you.

DAILY PRACTICE

Clear roles will ease the tension in the classroom; students will understand your expectations and you will fulfill them. Which role is most important to you? Does it affect you, as a teacher? Does it have an impact on your students?

Help your students understand and become aware of their roles.

Reference to p. 66
Daily One Minute Meditation

DAY 28

TAKE INITIATIVE: ADDRESS THE CONCERN

In order to become aware of your inner and outer conflicts, we have addressed two topics: emotions and the five core concerns. Let's review how these may influence your behavior when conflicts arise.

Imagine a conflict stirring up inside you. For example, you have a student, Joseph, who interrupts class by throwing paper balls at his classmates. Now, imagine a bale of hay. It needs only one spark to light the fire and start the blaze. That spark – Joseph's action – ignites your flame. Here are some scenarios of how you might react:

1. You identify your emotions with the spark and the flame at the same time, starting the blaze. Your body becomes tense and you respond with a violent reaction. You say: *"I am so furious!"* or *"I am so disappointed!"*

2. You make a difference between the spark and the flame. You become aware of your emotions and exclaim: *"Joseph, I feel angry right now."* or *"I feel disappointed."*

3. You identify the flame with one of the Five Core Concerns. You pause to think this through. The flame – the anger – is minimized because you are thinking of your status through the five concerns. This pause helps you take care of yourself. You are able to analyze the root of the problem instead of the emotion caused by his actions. This way, you release the inner pressure. In this case, your status has been compromised by Joseph's actions. You have rules in the classroom, and Joseph did not respect those rules. Eventually, you may say, *"Joseph, what would you say if everybody threw paper balls*

your way? Let's talk after class to see what the problem is and how we can solve it together."

In the first and second situation, the teacher was dealing with the emotions and not with the core concerns. In the first situation, she released her anger by reacting to the demanding situation, and, in the second situation, she recognized how she felt and expressed her anger. The third situation made the difference when she identified the concern: the lack of her status in the classroom. The solution she found was to invite Joseph for a talk after class. The way she acted in this conflict situation reinforced her status and minimized the emotions involved. Therefore, rather than focus on so many emotions, use the concerns to address the problem. Consequently, you can stimulate positive emotions both in yourself and in others.

Spark and Flame – Address the Concern

Consider these two suggestions when facing a difficult situation:

- Take the initiative. If you are dealing with someone in a difficult situation, do not wait for emotions to explode or overflow and then react. Think about Mr. Appreciation.

He could have taken the initiative and dealt with his status or affiliation with the other staff members. He could have also considered his role and asked for clarity. He could have used many options.

- Address the concern, not the emotion. In the situation presented in the story, as well as in any other situation, you want to mindfully focus on Status, Appreciation, Affiliation, Autonomy, or Role. Ms. Status, who was emotionally drained after her surgery and illness, could have addressed her need for affiliation with the others. Her concerns are not completely distinct from one another. They blend, mix, and merge. But each has its own special contribution in stimulating emotions.

DAILY PRACTICE

Think of a difficult situation you couldn't solve. Recall your emotions at that time. How did you react to that situation? Which of the Five Core Concerns triggered that situation? How would you address that concern now that you've identified it? What are your emotions now?

You may use this trail of thought as a pattern to address future challenging situations.

Reference to p. 66
Daily One Minute Meditation

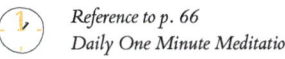

DAY 29

EMBRACE THE FIVE CORE CONCERNS

Clearly, emotions are at the core of your behavior. They make you feel either good or bad and are often the key to your actions. Emotions are signals you have in your body and mind telling you what is really going on with you. Thousands of emotions exist but it is impossible to deal with all of them. The staff's emotions in the Story of the Five Core Concerns were extreme. They ranged from sadness, to anger, fear, and impatience. How do you address your emotions? You will accept the Five Core Concerns that can help you focus on the problem, rather than become overwhelmed with the emotions themselves.

We will further summarize each core concern and review the consequences when one concern is ignored and when the same concern is addressed.

APPRECIATION:

When you feel unappreciated, your thoughts, feelings, and actions create negative reactions towards yourself and the people around you. On the other hand, when you feel appreciated, your thoughts, feelings and actions generate positive energy.

AFFILIATION:

When you do not have affiliation with your students, they may treat you as their adversary and keep you at a distance. But when you have affiliation with them, your chances of being treated with respect and warmth are much greater. You will enjoy your students for their uniqueness and they will appreciate you.

AUTONOMY:

When you don't have autonomy, your students may question your words and actions. They may not listen to you. When you have autonomy, your students will respect you and trust your decisions. Trust is a key factor in the learning process.

STATUS:

When your students are not treating you fairly, this may cause discipline problems in a disruptive classroom. When your status is met, you are given the recognition you deserve. You also want your students to get the recognition they deserve so that they feel valued.

ROLE:

When your roles are not clarified or are unfulfilling, you are not satisfied. This causes tension in the classroom. When they are fulfilling and clearly defined, your needs are being met! This goes for your students too. You want them to understand their roles and find them fulfilling. They will learn more and feel better about themselves.

DAILY PRACTICE

Reread the story and replace one of the characters with yourself. Choose a character whose behavior mirrors your own emotions in a similar situation. Which of the Core Concerns was triggered in that situation?

In a different scenario, the main characters are your students. Which students need appreciation from you or from their peers? By asking similar questions about the other core concerns, you will help your students identify their own emotions and find effective ways to deal with them successfully.

Reference to p. 66
Daily One Minute Meditation

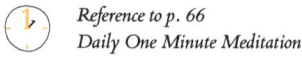

DAY 30

PRACTICE AFFIRMATIONS

In Chapter Two, *Recognize Your Thoughts*, you focused on your thoughts and related judgments. Chapter Three, *Be Aware of Your Emotions*, addressed the emotions connected to these thoughts, and you found ways to deal with them to reach a positive outcome. Practicing daily affirmations can improve your awareness of your emotions and help you focus on well-being. Affirmations help you reinforce positive thinking, creating new patterns that will add value to your life.

Reflect on the following affirmations:

I enjoy my status as a teacher.

I take responsibility for my role.

I build affiliation with my colleagues.

I show appreciation to my students.

I choose to address the concerns not the emotions.

DAILY PRACTICE

Take one affirmation and use it today to help you deal with your emotions.

Reference to p. 66
Daily One Minute Meditation

Notes

resilient

positive routines teacher

respect resilience forgiveness

goals bounce forward service

engagement HEART actions

focus learn from mistakes

persistence

values vision

positive self-talk commitment

challenge courage love

responsibility letting go

LEVEL THREE

ACTIONS

actions

CHAPTER FOUR

THE MINDFUL TEACHER

In this chapter, you will focus on actions to empower your skills and to become mindful of your students' needs. These actions reinforce the concepts detailed through the Levels of Awareness and Recognition. You gain self-awareness through these actions and because of this added awareness, you fill your life with the desire for personal growth. Your self-discovery brings meaning into your life. As you continue with these actions, you may experience healthier thoughts and emotions, and you may even realize you have a more positive attitude. This leads to self-respect and respect for your students. Thus, *The Teacher Within* creates a paradigm shift for you to take responsibility for your life, ultimately gaining fulfillment and happiness.

Your inner changes not only add fulfillment and more happiness for you, they can influence the mood of your entire classroom. A growth mindset challenges your students to perform and learn from their mistakes.

Becoming a mindful teacher is not a destination but rather a process, where you might face challenges. Our recommendation is to perform your Daily Practice and One Minute Meditation regularly; don't do too much at one time. You don't want to feel overwhelmed. These small changes will lead you to big gains.

Through days 31 to 40, you learn specific skills leading to actions you can take to become mindful. The following tips and tools may be handy for creating your mindful day:

Day 31. Begin the Day with Conscious Breathing

Day 32. Pause When You Are Overwhelmed

Day 33. Walk into the Classroom with a Positive Attitude Each

Day 34. Teach with Kindness

Day 35. Communicate with Mindful Body Language

Day 36. Be Aware of Your Listening Habits

Day 37. Use the Five Core Concerns as a Lens and a Lever to Build Relationships

Day 38. Choose Simplicity and Slow Down

Day 39. Keep an Open Mind

Day 40. End the Day with a Positive Routine

DAY 31

BEGIN THE DAY WITH CONSCIOUS BREATHING

At the beginning of the book, you became aware of your breath, instead of taking it for granted, as many of us do. Your breath may have lowered your stress levels and helped you focus and be mindful of the present moment. This may have become a habit but it can take a lifetime of practice.

Now, you will take the breathing practice to the next level and incorporate it in your daily routine. We call this *conscious breathing* because you connect your imagination with your breath. You are aware of your breath when you can imagine how the air enters your body and goes to places where you feel tension or pain. It's a conscious breathing process, directing your breath to the place where you feel the tension, slowly exhaling it, while getting rid of the tension and bringing your positive energy back. If you have a headache, pain or distress, you can try conscious breathing to regain your state of well-being. Tell yourself, "*I can breathe in positive energy.*" You consciously want to pay attention to the air entering your body and exiting through your mouth or nostrils.

Clare, a high-school Spanish teacher, asked us for advice. She said, *"Teaching is exhausting. I need to try something helpful."* We asked her to spend one minute in the morning focusing consciously on her breath and another minute in the evening before she went to bed. Clare replied, *"Seriously? But how can one minute of breathing help me?"* She was skeptical.

We asked her to have faith and try it for a couple of weeks. We always recommend doing the exercise for just one minute at a time. Our research and experience have consistently shown shorter practice times are better since they allow you to bypass your fears and worries. You aren't putting pressure on yourself by doing something for only one minute, so it isn't adding stress to your daily life.

She trusted us and continued her practice. Clare became aware of her breathing and realized how uneven her breath became when she was angry, stressed, or concerned. She returned two weeks later and said, *"I'm so excited about my success; I can already feel the change in the way I perceive the daily events. I decided to do one more minute of conscious breathing during the day!"* She was doing one-minute breathing exercises three times every day, once in the morning, once at lunch time, and once in the evening. Within the next few months, she noted a marked difference in her stress levels and this affected her attitude positively. She was impressed with the results she saw in her own life, so she introduced the practice to her students.

Consider setting up a routine to start your day with a breathing exercise. One-minute breathing reconnects you with the light of the day, the nature, and everything positive around you. It lowers your stress at the beginning of the day. Consider adding it to your morning routine. It is a great way to start your day feeling energized, and it takes only one minute.

You can also do a one-minute breathing exercise in the classroom, before your students arrive so you are relaxed and ready to teach.

DAILY PRACTICE

In the morning, when you wake up, your mind is clear and settled. Take advantage of this moment and start your day with a one-minute breathing exercise. Be observant of the present moment. Watch your floating thoughts drift through your mind. Set the tone for the day.

One-minute breathing can help students focus on their tasks and perform at their best. Consider teaching this practice to your students so they can practice it before exams, different contests, stage performance, games, etc.

Daily One Minute Meditation

ONE MINUTE MEDITATION FOR CHAPTER 4

Find a comfortable seated position.

Close your eyes or lower your gaze.

Rest your hands in your lap, palms up.

Bring your awareness to your breath.

Inhale through your nose for 4 counts.

Exhale through your mouth for 6 counts.

Think of your first day practicing mindfulness.

Reflect on your thoughts and emotions.

Imagine you are a mindful teacher.

You bring happiness to your students.

Inhale through your nose for 4 counts.

Exhale through your mouth for 6 counts.

Repeat this breathing pattern for 4 times.

Smile as you slowly open your eyes.

DAY 32

PAUSE WHEN YOU ARE OVERWHELMED

It is natural to have times during your day when your mind is overwhelmed with thoughts, emotions and judgments. The normal tendency is to push through it all and, somehow, keep going even though those emotions are still with you; you are on autopilot. When you're set on autopilot, you feel the heaviness pushing down your shoulders and, eventually, you will feel exhausted.

Besides conscious breathing, we can also approach times of stress and tension with a short *pause*. *Pause* can become a tool that helps a mindful teacher to become grounded and move forward through the day with clear intentions.

You may consider taking a *pause* when you feel overwhelmed and recognize a difficult situation. There are moments when you lose your confidence, become self-critical and judgmental. A *pause* can help you break the tension, take better care of yourself and think your reaction through before you act.

Reflect on the following questions when you are overwhelmed:

- What's going on that makes me feel this way?
- Is it my class, my students or other issues in my life?

A *pause* gives you awareness of the situation and anchors you to the present moment. It inserts a space between your emotions and your actions, helping you to respond in a mindful way.

Whatever the situation may be, you have the choice to take a pause to evaluate things. You may not have the time to leave the room, but a simple pause gives you the space to think through, recognize your need, and take action.

When you allow your mind to carry burdens, your body responds with fatigue. You will find a mere 15-second *pause* will make all the difference. The difficult situation will become less intimidating and, most likely, you will feel composed. Adding a *pause* leads you to positive actions.

DAILY PRACTICE

Identify a difficult situation during your teaching day. Commit to take a pause and focus on your breath.

Do you feel the difference when you pause for one minute?

Share this practice with your students and ask them to observe how it affects their stress levels.

Reference to p. 97
Daily One Minute Meditation

DAY 33

WALK INTO THE CLASSROOM WITH A POSITIVE ATTITUDE EACH DAY

Have you ever thought about how your attitude can influence the mood of the whole classroom? Odds are unhappy teachers with a negative attitude will spread their mood to the entire class, making their students unhappy. Now, imagine positive and enthusiastic teachers in their classrooms, spreading their positive attitude to students to set the tone for the day.

Let's examine the effects of the following two scenarios. Only the last few sentences are different. Yet, they set the mood for the day.

Scenario 1: I wake up exhausted on this gray, rainy morning, after an argument last night with my spouse about our finances. Agitated and frustrated, I get out of bed and go straight to the kitchen to make omelets and oatmeal for the kids. The boys come in and gobble down their food. Shortly, our daughter walks in and says, *"You know I hate oatmeal. I won't eat it!"* My spouse enters looking irritable. He says, *"I can't take the kids to school, a meeting has come up. You'll have to take them today."* I shift into gear for the change of plans, get dressed, take the kids to school, and barely make it to my classroom on time. As I enter, I feel a surge of anger rise up in me. I say loudly: *"Everybody in your seats. We'll start the class now!"* And I start the school day with a negative attitude, with the students looking gloomy and wondering what they did to deserve such a welcome.

Scenario 2: I wake up exhausted on this gray, rainy morning, after an argument last night with my spouse about our finances. Agitated and frustrated, I get out of bed and go straight to the kitchen to make omelets and oatmeal for the kids. The boys come in and gobble down the food. Our daughter walks in shortly thereafter and says, *"You know I hate oatmeal. I won't eat it!"* My spouse enters the kitchen looking edgy. He says, *"I can't take the kids to school, a meeting has come up. You'll have to take them today."* I shift gears for the change of plans, get dressed, take the kids to school, and barely make it to my class on time. As I enter the classroom, I take a deep breath, get focused on my class, smile, and say, *"Good morning, everyone. Let's greet each other and enjoy the day. It's great to see you all here!"* The students smile back and start the day on a positive note.

DAILY PRACTICE

Which of the two scenarios would be your response?

Why have you chosen this scenario?

Recognize how you feel before you walk into your classroom. Take one positive emotion and choose to let it guide you throughout your day. Think of a statement you would like to make to your students and set the tone for the day.

Reference to p. 97
Daily One Minute Meditation

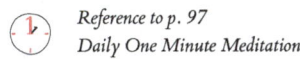

DAY 34

TEACH WITH KINDNESS

Kindness is a two-way street. If you are kind and treat others with kindness, chances are they will respond to you the same way. Kindness is known as a barrier breaker, may it be hate, anger, or frustration. Share thoughts or words of kindness as a reward for the relations you have with your students. They may not remember all the facts you teach, but they will always remember the times when you were kind to them. This way you let them know that you are there to listen, respect and care for them.

Joan, a biology teacher said, *"When I think about my life as a teacher for over 30 years, the most important word I can think of is kindness. It reflects what I wanted from my students and what I needed within myself. The times were challenging and my students coming from different backgrounds were full of anger and frustration, which manifested very often in their behavior as they bullied each other, offending even the teachers. I realized that something had to be done, so I tried various methods to improve the atmosphere and the relations between my students. However, there was this one middle school class where nothing worked. I decided to try an experiment with them: I suggested that we cultivate kindness. We took two pots and planted the same seeds of flowers to be grown by the students. On one of the pots we wrote: "We care for you" and we didn't write anything on the other pot. The students had to take turns in watering the plants while keeping one rule in mind: when they watered the first plant with the tag "we care for you," they had to say words of kindness and appreciation. When watering the other plant, they did not need to do anything. Even if we didn't concentrate on the result, we were lucky to see the astonishing outcome: the first plant which received words and thoughts of kindness was the first one to spring up and grow faster and taller than the second one. This was an extraordinary lesson for my hardly manageable students. They saw with their own eyes how kindness can benefit growth. Our project created the framework for bringing kindness into the classroom. The children made a list with the words of kindness used while caring for the flower to grow. When I think back to those days, I remember seeing the effects immediately. They started using the same words of kindness among each other and they grew friendships and good relations. I was more enthusiastic in the classroom and it helped me as much as it helped them."*

When you practice kindness, you become more committed to your students. You value each one of them in a different way. When you are kind, your actions make your students feel good. They will smile and recognize your kindness. You get immediate feedback. You affect the lives of your students positively and build a community within your classroom. Add kindness to your teaching practice to achieve huge gains!

"I care for you" flower pot - Teach with kindness

DAILY PRACTICE

Practice Joan's philosophy of kindness: in the morning, start your day with an act of kindness. Set an intention to do something kind for one student and then carry it out.

Reference to p. 97
Daily One Minute Meditation

DAY 35

COMMUNICATE WITH MINDFUL BODY LANGUAGE

Communication, both verbal and non-verbal, is one of the most important tools in any relation. Mindful teachers are aware of the importance of good communication with their students, building it on a foundation of kindness, understanding, attention, and compassion.

Communication built on this foundation brings along feelings expressed in the way you speak, supported by your posture, gestures and facial expressions. A mindful body language opens the door to mindful communication. Be aware of your body language; it is an important tool to learn about your thoughts and emotions.

When you trust yourself, you have a posture of confidence, you sit or stand up straight and your gestures are open. You keep good eye contact and you are aware that your facial expressions reflect your feelings. On the other hand, when you don't trust yourself, your body bends forward, your gestures are closed, and it can be difficult to make eye-contact.

As a mindful teacher, you become aware of the feelings expressed by your students' body language and of how interested, involved, and focused they are during class. This helps you adapt your teaching and keep them curious and involved.

Think about how your body language appears to your students. Consider the following tips for a mindful communication:

1. Walk into the classroom with your back straight and a smile on your face.

2. Keep good eye contact while you teach.

3. Nod your head and show signals that you listen to them.

4. Think about where you usually keep your arms and support your message with hand gestures. Crossed arms do not reflect open communication; however, relaxed at your side do.

The spark in your students' eyes is the sign of effective communication.

DAILY PRACTICE

Be aware of how you walk into the classroom at the beginning of each class. Make a commitment to step in with a posture of confidence and trust. Welcome your students with your shoulders straight, your chin raised instead of pointing down, and a smile on your face. Set up a positive atmosphere from the very beginning of the lesson.

Reference to p. 97
Daily One Minute Meditation

DAY 36

BE AWARE OF YOUR LISTENING HABITS

Refresh your listening skills. You discover more about yourself when you become aware of how you listen to your students, of the tone of your voice, and of how you resonate with your students. Observe your students' facial expression, their body language and listen to their voices. Your improved listening skills will enhance your self-awareness.

Margaret, a middle-school math teacher, never thought about her listening skills until Fred, her student, raised his voice to her one day, *"Miss, you aren't listening to me. I am trying to tell you I don't understand the math and you are ignoring me. I am going to fail the test."*

Those aren't words we want to hear from our students. And they certainly weren't respectful, but there was a strong message in the statement. Margaret was wise enough to hear it. She sat down with Fred and asked him to talk more about his problem. It wasn't easy for her, but she said, *"Fred, tell me what's the problem. I am here to listen."* He replied bluntly, *"You don't look at me or at my colleagues when you talk to us. You never wait until we finish the question; you don't even listen when we ask you something. We're all scared we will fail our exam!"* Margaret was stunned! Focusing on her teaching and covering all the topics was certainly important. She had no idea her listening skills were so poor. She felt offended and embarrassed and decided to look for help to improve her listening skills.

She did a lot of research and designed a "Mindful Listening" personal program based a few simple rules:

1. Get ready to listen! Take a breath and focus.

2. Make eye-contact with the student who is speaking and don't get distracted by anything else. Let him/her know you are listening to what he/she is saying.

3. Listen to the tone of his/her voice and tune in to what is being said. Control the tone of your voice when you answer.

4. Do not interrupt even if it is difficult to allow the student to finish before you start speaking. Count to ten before you speak.

Margaret's teaching improved because she listened more closely and her days felt more satisfying.

Mindful listening helps your students develop a positive attitude towards learning and brings you the satisfaction of having made yourself understood.

DAILY PRACTICE

Look at Margaret's suggestions for better listening skills. Reflect on your own listening skills and find the areas you need to improve. Make a commitment to listen mindfully whenever you communicate with your students.

Reference to p. 97
Daily One Minute Meditation

DAY 37

USE THE FIVE CORE CONCERNS AS A LENS AND A LEVER TO BUILD RELATIONSHIPS

In Level Two, *Recognition*, you were introduced to the Five Core Concerns: a constructive way to use your emotions to improve your relations with students and colleagues. Every day, you face emotions produced by internal and external factors. Often, negative behavior has nothing to do with you. Conflicts can arise at any moment. How you deal with them makes all the difference. You may have a student who has low self-esteem, feels a sense of powerlessness and is defiant. His attitude and the way he reacts to challenges can bring on dysfunctions in the classroom, which can grow into conflicts.

You can use the Five Core Concerns as a lens to help you understand which concern is not met so you can tailor your actions to address them. Let's say you walk into your classroom and the students are out of control. Use the Five Core Concerns as a checklist of sensitive areas to look for in yourself and in your students. You might ask yourself:

In what ways might my students feel that their *status* is being compromised? Am I making them feel good about themselves? Or do they feel as though they have no *autonomy*? Do I tell them what to do all of the time and give them no chance to make their own choices? Or do they need to *affiliate* with one another? Did they have time to talk with their peers and get their input? Do they feel *unappreciated* for their efforts when I ignored their plea for less homework? You can use your questions to understand the current situation.

You can also use the Five Core Concerns as a lever to help improve a situation. You can lower the tension in the classroom when you stimulate positive emotions based on the core concern that you feel needs to be addressed. You can say, *"For the next hour, you are going to have free time to do what you want to do. Now, you must abide by the rules and not leave the room, and you must talk quietly; this is time for you to reconnect with your classmates, or take time for yourself."* This is giving them status, affiliation, autonomy; you are appreciating them and accepting positive behavior. All of this is done without changing the roles you have as teacher and student.

The Five Core Concerns are human wants that are important to you and every one of your students. Use them both as a lens and a lever to help your students feel good about themselves while you also have your needs met.

DAILY PRACTICE

Think of a class situation. Make it a specific situation when you had a difficult time. Now look at the Five Core Concerns as a lens to examine the situation more clearly. How could the Five Core Concerns have helped you prepare, conduct, and review the emotional dimensions of this situation?

Once you have examined the concerns through a lens, then think about how they can be used as a lever to help improve the situation. How could you have used them to shift the emotions in a positive direction? Which concerns were unmet?

The following questions will help you use the Five Core Concerns both as a lens and a lever; grade your answers on a scale from 1 to 5.

What number have you circled? What does it mean for you?

APPRECIATION

- Do you show appreciation to your students?

1 2 3 4 5

- Do you feel appreciated by your students?

1 2 3 4 5

AUTONOMY

- Do you give your students autonomy whenever possible?

1 2 3 4 5

- Do you feel autonomy when you work with your students?

1 2 3 4 5

AFFILIATION

- Do your students bond with you and each other?

  1 2 3 4 5

- How attached do you feel to your students?

  1 2 3 4 5

STATUS

- Do you make sure your students have status?

  1 2 3 4 5

- To what extent do you feel you express respect towards your students?

  1 2 3 4 5

ROLE

- Are you clear about your roles?

  1 2 3 4 5

- Do your students know and understand your role and theirs in the classroom?

  1 2 3 4 5

Reference to p. 97
Daily One Minute Meditation

DAY 38

CHOOSE SIMPLICITY AND SLOW DOWN

When you teach with simplicity, you don't cram too much into one day. You think about what is important for you and you follow your own truth. If you are mindful, you are aware that only an uncluttered mind can stay focused on the present moment and make the most of it.

We live in a world full of information and products. At every step, we are bombarded with commercials, and we accumulate more and more possessions. Pause for a minute and reflect. Will having all of these items bring you more happiness? Or are you likely to become frustrated and end up with a cluttered mind?

Once you become aware of the clutter in your classroom, you may feel the stress in your body and the desire to get back in control. Clean and declutter your home or your classroom and let go of some of your attachments. This can be difficult, but the results are worth it. You will be making a genuine commitment to what is important to you and what brings value to you. When you become able to let go of things, you allow compassion and gratitude to enter your life. It helps you slow down and focus on your students' needs.

When you choose simplicity, you automatically slow down. Your lessons will be meaningful and comprehensive and will bring along the joy of learning. Embrace simplicity for a more fulfilling teaching experience.

The first thing you can do to reduce the clutter in your mind is to focus on your breath. This automatically brings you in the present moment, reduces your stress, and allows you to become calmer, less distracted, and more focused.

Jenna, a first-grade teacher, was overwhelmed. She had too much to do, her classroom was cluttered and so was her mind. Her first-grade students were disruptive and often out of control. She told us, *"I wondered what I could do. I looked around in my cluttered classroom and decided to give away things I do not need such as the old books. I asked my students to declutter their desks and to keep only things that meant anything to them. The environment in my classroom changed and had a positive impact on my students. I learned that simplicity is not an easy choice, and I realized that less can become more."*

DAILY PRACTICE

When you enter your classroom, look around as if you were there for the first time. Become aware of what you see, what you like, and what you would like to change.

How can you achieve greater simplicity?

Reference to p. 97
Daily One Minute Meditation

DAY 39

KEEP AN OPEN MIND

Learning is a quest for knowledge and personal development. If your mindset is flexible, you believe in your abilities and your mind is open to new things. You find pleasure in what you do; as a result, your involvement and energy level increase. You value teaching and learning and you are open to continuous development.

A mindful teacher will always find his/her own truth, stay constructive, and avoid trying to look smart in order to impress. If you, as a teacher, learn from your mistakes and look at them as opportunities to grow and improve, your students will likely follow the same model. Find ways to embrace your challenges and look at them as opportunities to keep your motivation alive. If your students perform poorly, do not look at the weaknesses; try to find their strengths and help them grow.

You teach your students to value their learning and you appreciate the effort they make, leading them to achievements and strengthening their perseverance. They will learn they don't have to be perfect.

An open mind is less judgmental and has no boundaries. When you take your time to pause and reflect, you allow yourself to get answers from within. If you teach your students to make choices and allow them to fail, they will learn not to let fear stop them and move on.

Sandra, a middle school counselor, suggested that her students imagine the following scenario when they have to make difficult choices in their lives. She told them, "*Imagine that you are in a box, safely protected from the dangers of the outside world. You move around inside this box but your actions and decisions are all limited within the walls. There are no windows or doors. You are safe because you are inside your box, but you feel that you cannot grow or do anything extraordinary. You have to stay inside your limitations.*

Now imagine you have the courage to open your box and explore new things outside your safe zone. It's a big world out there, but it takes courage to step out and explore it. You can count only on your strengths and determination. Will you take the step out?"

Every time a student faces fears of choices, Sandra turns back to the model of the box and asks the student to open his box and imagine the situation with unlimited opportunities outside his box. She tells them: *"It's your box, so it's your responsibility to open the lid and make your choice. I trust you will make the best decision."* Sandra was a mindful teacher who encouraged her students to have an open mind, connect to the world, and rely on their strengths to explore it.

The box: Imagine that you are in a box – Keep an open mind

DAILY PRACTICE

Go back to Sandra's box. "*Imagine that you are in the same box, safely protected from the dangers of the outside world that you described to your students. You move around inside this box but your actions and decisions are all limited within the walls of the box. There are no windows or doors. You are safe because you are stuck inside your box, but you feel you cannot grow or do anything extraordinary.*

Now imagine you have the courage to open your box and explore new things outside your safe zone. It's a big world out there, but it takes courage to step out and explore it. You can only count on your strengths and determination. Will you step out? What will you do?"

Reference to p. 97
Daily One Minute Meditation

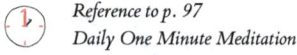

DAY 40

END THE DAY WITH A POSITIVE ROUTINE

The end of your school day is as important as the beginning of the day. You want to end on a positive note. This allows you to leave the class with a sense of joy and it also gives the students the same message. *"We've had a great day!"*

Sometimes, at the end of the day, you may feel exhausted. This may happen to your students as well. Whatever you do to bring positive energy back to the classroom can help you and your students anticipate the next activity with excitement.

We will call this reflection time. It is the moment when you bring your attention to your breathing and pause for 30 seconds.

Ask your students to reflect on the day. Ask them to focus on their breathing and think about the best moments of the day. Be an example for them and pause in the same way you ask them to do. Reflection time helps your students focus on their needs. This is the time when you all are present in the *here* and *now*. You know what feels right. When you end with a smile, you know you have done well.

DAILY PRACTICE

Form a new routine at the end of your school day. Make sure you meet your needs and those of your students. Get their input or ask a colleague for suggestions.

There is no right or wrong way to create this routine, as long as it satisfies you and your students and brings closure to the day in a positive way.

Reference to p. 97
Daily One Minute Meditation

CHAPTER FIVE

THE RESILIENT TEACHER

Over the past 40 days, you have been building mindfulness skills, which we hope have begun to ease your life and also affect your students positively. Now, we stress the importance of resilience since it is a key factor of success in the classroom.

As a resilient teacher, you will gain the strength and the ability to overcome challenges in your classroom. You will be able to confront such challenges even when they lie outside your comfort zone. No matter the circumstances, this chapter will give you tools so you can rise above your hesitations and get the task done. You will aim to become the best of who you are.

These are essential tools for every teacher. For the next ten days, you will focus on the skills that build resilience within you. Each skill gives you an increased sense of self-awareness. You will critically analyze your attitude and perspective on various situations so you are prepared to deal with the unknown when it occurs. Since no two people are alike and we all have our differences, you can create your unique path based on the information you find most important.

Your journey toward becoming a resilient teacher starts right now for ten days:

Day 41. Create a Vision

Day 42. Bounce Forward

Day 43. Forgive Yourself in the Face of Adversity

Day 44. Rebuild a Better Version of Yourself

Day 45. Use Positive Self-Talk

Day 46. Use the Word "Challenge" Instead of "Problem"

Day 47. Engage with Resilient and Mindful People

Day 48. Show Courage and Commitment

Day 49. Be Always at the Top of Your Game

Day 50. Build a Mindset for Bouncing Forward

DAY 41

CREATE A VISION

To be prepared for everyday situations, you need a plan and goals, and you need to know your material thoroughly so you can teach at your best. When you focus on a vision, it becomes the driving force toward successful teaching. Your vision is born from your passion, dreams, and wishes. It helps you accomplish your daily tasks and keeps your energy and enthusiasm alive.

Defining your vision starts with reflecting on what you want to accomplish in the long term. When you have a strong vision, you will feel it strongly in your mind and heart. It will bring positive energy and power into your life, giving you the strength to wake up every morning and accomplish it. Writing it down brings you more power than just thinking about it. To emphasize motivation and success, you will use the present tense when you write your purposeful vision.

Your vision is supported by your goals. Each goal has to be carried out with commitment and determination. These will help you achieve your vision no matter the circumstances. You will surely have both good days and difficult ones. With commitment and determination, you can achieve your vision through them all.

Let's consider daily goals. Start by asking yourself, *"What do I want to accomplish today?"* Your goals have to be simple, specific, and easy to achieve in order to keep up your motivation. The goals should include:

- Specific details of what you want to accomplish daily.
- Measurable targets, with a beginning and an end.
- Important, but not urgent, tasks.

A goal could be, *"Today, I want to be present when I teach." or "I will be aware of my breathing before I start each class."* Your actions support the achievement of your goals and vision.

In the early 1990s, Simona lived in Romania, a country where the state schools' regimented curriculum of the now defunct communist regime left no room for creative and innovative teaching methods. Simona envisioned opening a school to bring radical change to the Romanian education system. *Her vision was to open her own school with a new approach to education.*

In order to achieve her vision, she set her first goal: to start a small kindergarten. Besides being a full-time teacher and mother of two, she needed to do more to achieve her goal. At the beginning, her goal was to make five toys a day. She worked methodically at this task. Each day she showed success by finishing five toys. Soon, she made $70 and purchased the first tables and chairs. She focused on her vision and, after several months, opened the kindergarten in her family's small apartment. Twelve children enrolled, and her goal of five toys a day was already a success. Over the years, Simona's goals changed but her vision never wavered. In 2004, when the school was still at the beginning of its journey, with 110 students enrolled, Simona wrote her vision on a piece of paper: *"Our school is the best school in Romania."* Five years later, in 2009, the school became the first "School of the Year in Romania." Today, it is a pre-k through 12th grade school, with over 700 students enrolled, with its own campus, and it is considered a role model for education in Romania.

Simona envisioned a school for change and she followed her dream. She planned and was well-prepared, and, most importantly, she had the drive to succeed. Whenever she looked into her heart, she always found her vision as her internal driving force. Her small goals, which may have seemed insignificant to some people, grew into huge gains.

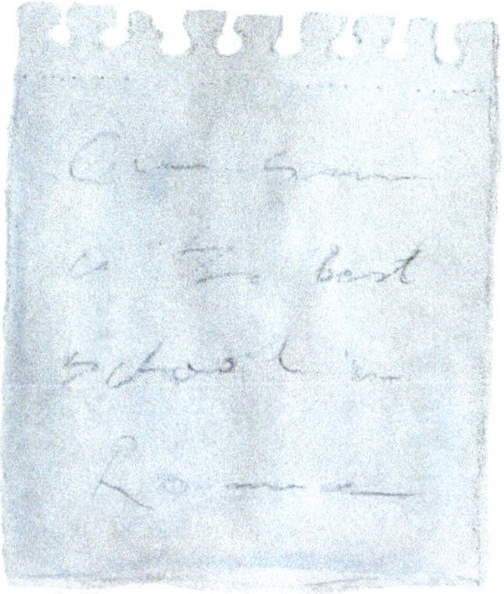

"Our school is the best school in Romania" – Vision

DAILY PRACTICE

Think of your vision. Write it down so that you can turn it into reality. Remember: your vision is a picture of your teaching now and in the future, with inspiration and a framework.

Once you have written it down, read it out loud. Close your eyes and imagine your vision is fulfilled. How do you feel? When you open your eyes, think of the first goal you want to accomplish.

To build resilience remember to set your goal with commitment and determination.

Daily One Minute Meditation

ONE MINUTE MEDITATION FOR CHAPTER 5

Create your own vision.

Imagine it is written on a whiteboard.

Imagine you have accomplished your vision.

What are your feelings when you enjoy your accomplishment?

Hold these feelings deep in your heart.

These feelings will give you the power of resilience whenever you need it.

Inhale through your nose for 4 counts.

Exhale through your mouth for 6 counts.

Repeat this breathing pattern for 4 times.

Smile as you slowly open your eyes.

DAY 42

BOUNCE FORWARD!

This is a day dedicated to one of the main skills of resilience: bouncing back. The story of Eli C., a 19-year-old student at the University of Pennsylvania Wharton Business School, helped us rephrase this skill, from bouncing back to bouncing forward. This is his letter:

"When people talk about resilience, they often define it as something along the lines of: "being able to bounce back from adversity." In fact, for most of my life, if you had asked me to define resilience, this is the definition I would have shared with you.

However, during my junior year of high school, everything changed. My mother unexpectedly passed away. Unfortunately, it wouldn't be the last loss that year - my grandmother and my aunt passed away both within 6 months after my mother. These losses crushed me, and, for a period of time, I felt I was completely alone.

In my environmental studies class, we discussed about natural disasters. When a town or city is destroyed, one of three things happens: the city is either destroyed beyond recovery, it will slowly recover to where it was before, or it will use the destruction as an opportunity to rebuild everything better than it was before. I've come to realize this is also true for people when they're struck by a personal tragedy.

When I lost my Mom, I was completely crushed. She was my rock, my "go-to," and one of the only people and the only person I felt like I could really be myself when she was around. My entire foundation had been destroyed and, as I looked around at my life, I honestly didn't know if I would ever recover. Like a city struck by a natural disaster, I slowly began to pick up the pieces. The process wasn't fast, but I was able to use this tragedy to completely rebuild who I was as a person. I was able to build a better version of myself – I "bounced forward," and I learned in those moments that, if a hurricane hits my life, I can use it to rebuild a stronger foundation. I know this is what my mom would want, and I live every day to make her proud."

We know mothers have an impact on who we are. As teachers we don't always realize the impact that we can have on someone. Eli's words are directed toward his mother, but aren't we, as teacher also able to teach resilience? We asked Eli and here is his answer.

"When asked about the people who shaped me the most into the person I am today, I always think of my high school Student Government Advisor.

Educators really have a unique opportunity to touch students' lives and shape them as people. Students' needs will vary, but it's often as simple as taking time to listen to them and getting to know their needs. Nobody becomes resilient on their own and we all need someone we can go to in our moments of weakness. After losing my mother, I had days where just sitting in class was too much, and knowing I could reach out to my advisor just to get away was often enough.

Personally, I can't thank my teachers enough. My teachers taught me so much more than the curriculum in their classes, and they're a significant part of who I am today. I'd like to take a moment to thank all the educators who supported me through the most difficult years of my life and made me the man I am today. As students, we never thank you enough, but we are truly grateful for everything you do."

Those are powerful words! Let's look at what Eli said because bounce forward is the most important skill to build resilience when circumstances are tough. Every teacher will encounter challenges in life and in the classroom. Daily challenges vary, such as a lesson not going the way it was planned, a student who is facing a crisis, or a meeting with an unhappy parent; there are endless challenges in a teacher's day. As a teacher, you can't assume you know how things will turn out.

Conversations are essential to building resilience. There are lessons in just about any moment, and having a conversation to help students realize this is essential. Build a relationship with the student, and make sure they know they can come to you in their moments of stress. There's no single way to do this and it takes time, but it will give you the chance to build your students' trust.

When you *bounce forward*, you recognize what occurred, you deal with it and you learn from it. You don't give up. Imagine you are swimming in the ocean when the tide begins to pull you down. You feel as if you are drowning. Then, all of a sudden, someone drops a lifebuoy to save you. Now, it's your choice to grab it or let exhaustion take over. You may be exhausted and terrified, feeling like you don't have the strength to hold on. But your alternative is to drown. You push past your fears to gain the momentum in the water and you are saved! You don't rely on the negative – you create a stronger foundation within yourself – just like Eli did. This is an extreme situation but it is much like your mind. As a teacher, you will have challenges you must face. The question is, can you *bounce forward*? Your mind is your source of power - to *bounce forwa*rd in life when faced with difficult situations.

When something unexpected happens, adrenaline runs through your body and gives you a push to move on. It keeps you safe when you need it. But it can wreak havoc on your emotional and spiritual health if you don't know how to *bounce forwa*rd! If you panic, it acts as food for fear. If fear grows, you will never be able to catch your lifebuoy and move to safety.

Your first job is to be aware of your thoughts and reactions when a difficult situation occurs. Recognize those thoughts and take a deep breath. Think back to those times and recognize the resilience you had in past situations. Realize you have power over your thoughts this time too. Meditation can help relax your brain and find the power to bounce forward.

DAILY PRACTICE

If Eli could bounce forward after his mother's death to build a stronger foundation, you too can bounce forward. If Eli's mother gave him the desire to make her proud of him every day, you, as a teacher, can impact your students so every student is proud to have you as their teacher.

What do you do when things in your daily life happen differently from what you had hoped they could be?

What strategies do you use to quickly adapt to such a change?

How can you use Eli's story to help your students bounce forward?

Reference to p. 124
Daily One Minute Meditation

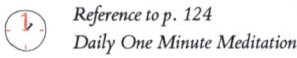

DAY 43

FORGIVE YOURSELF IN THE FACE OF ADVERSITY

Another skill for developing resilience is to forgive yourself and others, which follows your vision and ability to bounce forward. It takes courage because it involves how you think about yourself and how you deal with others in the face of adversity.

We all make mistakes in life. The important thing is to recognize when mistakes occur. You are then able to forgive and not judge or blame yourself. This does not mean you will not feel anger, sadness, or disappointment. It means you have the courage to forgive.

Forgiveness is a skill you must practice over time. It does not come overnight and it takes hard work. It includes mindfulness because it has its origin in your thoughts. Therefore, you must first awaken to forgiveness through mindfulness and then follow the resilient path of not giving up.

Forgiveness means you let go of the past, live in the present, and choose to believe in yourself. It is your mind that controls your ability to forgive. You accept the present and stop wishing you could change the past. If you feel the need to gain control over this part of the journey towards personal resilience, you might want to review Chapter Two "Recognizing Your Thoughts" and Chapter Three "Recognizing Your Emotions." When you practice forgiveness, you build mindfulness and resilient behavior.

Moira, a fourth-grade teacher, often had to deal with trauma in her life, and she believed it affected her teaching. She recalls, *"I can never forget the time my parents were fighting, and my Dad said he would divorce my Mom. I had to pretend I didn't hear them. It haunted me for years. I analyzed the situation over and over again. I had no control over my parents. I was a child. I realized about eight years ago that I never solved these issues. My parents stayed together until my Dad died, even though the fights continued. I lived with the fear of abandonment my whole life. I didn't trust adults. I was angry, and I felt it was all my fault. I found myself taking on the blame and guilt into my teaching and into my relationships. I often thought it was my fault when a student didn't succeed, or if I couldn't get along well with my husband. I know now, it was not my fault.*

Years later, when I met Simona and Susan, over many shared conversations, I realized I had to learn to forgive my parents for their relationship and I had to focus on the good days we spent together. I started to use breathing and meditation. I slowly came to the conclusion that mistakes are a part of our lives. I realized my father was begging for status and he didn't feel appreciated by my mom. And she in turn didn't feel like she had the autonomy she wanted. She wasn't able to work outside of the home because she was responsible for me and my five siblings. In fact, the Five Core Concerns *gave me insight into forgiveness and helped me understand more about myself and my parents; this process relieved the pressure of self-blame and negativity. Breathing exercises helped me release stress. I still work daily on the notion that I deserve to forgive myself, and it helps me when I forgive my parents and learn from these past mistakes. But I can't pretend it is an easy fix."*

Most people have been raised to believe making mistakes is wrong and, therefore, when they do make a mistake, they are devastated. Resilience means knowing how to cope with failure; nobody is perfect and failure can become part of your success!

DAILY PRACTICE

This reflection will start with a question: what has been bothering you for a long time?

It could be something that hurt you or something you have blamed yourself for years. It could be something that happened to you. Think about your feelings related to that experience.

Take five minutes to write a letter for yourself expressing your feelings and your concerns at that time. It should be a short, powerful letter to help you release your frustrations.

When you have finished your letter, you may say, "I forgive myself and I move on." Tear up the letter and forgive yourself.

Reference to p. 124
Daily One Minute Meditation

DAY 44

REBUILD A BETTER VERSION OF YOURSELF

Our past experiences influence all of us. Memories will remain in our minds and develop certain beliefs and thinking patterns. Negative memories will add stress to our lives. We carry them around like baggage that becomes heavier as time passes by. This baggage can harm us and even destroy us.

How can we learn from the memories of our past experiences to build our resilience?

Learn from those memories and build a stronger foundation. This is the time you can build resilience. This baggage can give you an understanding about yourself. You can learn from it. No matter how difficult it was, if you use it to gain something positive, it becomes useful to you.

Decide to say *stop* and put the baggage down. Realize you are carrying useless burdens and life isn't working for you this way. Resilience is the power within you to use that experience in a way that serves you best.

Learning from past experiences takes time though, and it is normal to feel the weight again. Through mindfulness techniques and meditation, you gain the chance to start a new journey with lighter baggage. Your baggage might feel heavy again over time, but now you are aware you must stop, think about what you have learned from it, and then move on. Build a better version of yourself.

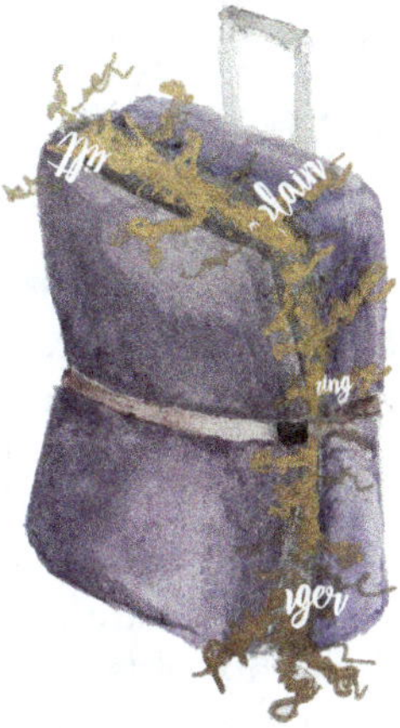

Your baggage – Resilience – Build a better version of yourself

DAILY PRACTICE

Take a pause for a moment and imagine the baggage you've been carrying along your road. Feel its weight. Now, open your baggage and look into it.

What are the first three things you notice?

Do they add value to your life?

If they don't, let go of them!

Pick up your lighter baggage and continue your journey!

Reference to p. 124
Daily One Minute Meditation

DAY 45

USE POSITIVE SELF-TALK

When you become aware of your thoughts, you start hearing your inner voice and listening to the words you use. The dominant voice is often the critical voice about yourself or about the actions you want to take. We all talk to ourselves during the day and, quite often, we choose the mantra "I can't do this" or "it's hard to do that." This creates a resistance in our minds, even before we start to take action. When we become aware of this inner voice, we can change the negative words with words of appreciation and encouragement. Cancel the negative words in your mind and, instead, consider positive self-talk or words of empowerment. Pay attention to your thoughts and recognize the words you use most often. This will help you anchor your thoughts to the present moment and set effective goals to accomplish by the end of the day.

The critical voice about yourself is connected to your emotions and feelings and prevents you from accomplishing your daily goals efficiently. It drains you energy. Replace negative thoughts with positive self-talk to counter negative messages. You can accomplish this new way of thinking by taking one small step at a time.

How can you create a positive and constructive self-talk once you have become aware of your thoughts and words?

You choose to stop the negative mantra and replace it with positive affirmations connected to the present moment. "I can't" becomes "I can" and "it's difficult" becomes "I can find solutions." When you shift your mindset, you will enjoy finding solutions.

You can give up words that don't serve you, such as: "hard," "impossible," "difficult" and start a list of positive words. Whatever those words may be, they will come from within you and become words of commitment to yourself.

These words empower and motivate you to build resilience within!

Joe, a middle school art teacher, explains it beautifully: *"Self-talk is what I say to myself over and over again, and ultimately defines who I am. It's the chatter in my mind which has shaped me in the past and continues to shape me. I have to make sure my self-talk is positive, and negative words don't take control. I talk to myself all the time, going over situations in my head and trying to determine the right path for me to take. These inner conversations are my ethical conscience."*

DAILY PRACTICE

Think of a recent situation that didn't feel right. Close your eyes and breathe for one minutes. Reflect on the following questions:

Are you aware of your self-talk? Yes/No

Take a piece of paper, fold it in two. On one side, write: "My critical voice says about me"; on the other side, change the critical words into constructive words and empower yourself with things you can do and act on.

Observe the pattern you use more often and focus on your positive self-talk.

What words will you include on your own self-talk list?

Share this exercise with your students.

Reference to p. 124
Daily One Minute Meditation

DAY 46

USE THE WORD "CHALLENGE" INSTEAD OF "PROBLEM"

Our mind is restricted or stimulated by the words we use. With negative words, you will make excuses and blame yourself. These words take your energy and enthusiasm away. The word *problem* seems innocent enough to use, but it is restrictive because it sets limits and has a negative connotation. Replace the word *problem* in your vocabulary with the word *challenge*. When you move from t *problem* to *challenge*, you break barriers and open up opportunities.

Today, use the word *challenge* and see how it feels. You will feel empowered to act and solve the situation. Your challenges will be less stressful and you will be able to focus on the outcome. You will be amazed at what a simple change in words can do!

Challenges improve resilience. The way you think about your challenges becomes the way you talk and act. In the first chapter, you learned about positive thinking and the effect it has on your mind, body, and soul. In a similar way, your challenges can impact your relations with fellow teachers and students. A resilient teacher is challenged by situations.

Let's look at Jill, a first-grade teacher.

Sue, her colleague, asked, *"How are you doing?"* Jill said, *"Great! My students are quite energetic and I have to put a lot of effort controlling them day by day. The problem is they don't listen to me but that's not unusual. They're just kids. I love teaching! My Dad is still in the hospital and the situation looks grim; the doctors don't want to tell me the truth; but I am okay. The Principal doesn't appreciate my work; he said I may not have a full time job next year because they are about to cut classes... But I don't care, I can deal with all these problems! Life is good!"*

Unfortunately, this is not the case with Jill and life is, in fact, not good at all! Jill's challenge is to be honest, not to blame others or play the role of the victim. She could have said, "There is a lot happening in my life right now. Still, I choose to look at the bright side and find opportunities in these challenges. My students are energetic, but I can deal with their behavior. I could take a workshop on hyperactivity in young children and learn more how to work with them. I could tell the doctor I need to know the truth about my father. The situation with the principal is indeed challenging, but I could reach out to him, asking for advice and help to keep my job; he needs to understand that my job is my life."

You can draw a fine line between the way you assess your situation and your willingness to look at circumstances as opportunities rather than challenges. Jill's life can improve and it will, eventually. But, at the present moment, recognize that, in life, everyone will have ups and downs. When we look at the down swings as challenges, we look at life from a different perspective and we can say, *"Life will be good."*

You want to focus on the positive aspects, despite the adversity you face. Resilience does not mean lying to yourself; it means you assume your responsibilities and you are true to yourself.

Be aware of your challenges. Focus on the reality of the situation so that you can use it to find the positive side of this challenge to boost your strengths and to become more resilient in the classroom and in your life.

DAILY PRACTICE

Reflect on the following questions, recognize your thoughts, and take action. You may want to write down your challenge and the solutions you find.

What has been your challenge today?

How can you state your challenge so that it is both truthful and positive?

Reference to p. 124
Daily One Minute Meditation

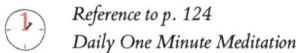

DAY 47

ENGAGE WITH RESILIENT AND MINDFUL PEOPLE

The skills you've acquired in this chapter facilitate the development of resilience from within. If you are mindful and resilient, you recognize the people who contribute to your life. None of us can live alone, we are all surrounded by people in the communities we live in. Some people may disappoint you or drain your energy with their negative attitude. You may try to change them, but always remember that the only person you can change is yourself; you can reflect on these relations and see what you can learn from every person you interact with. When it comes to building relationships, you have the freedom to choose whom you relate to. Choose to engage with people you can learn from and create trustful relations with.

During a seminar, we met three teachers who shared with us their stories:

Marta is a humanities teacher. She says, *"I choose to surround myself with people who are quite different. I learn from them. One of my colleagues is from Kenya; she believes in a different religion, her culture is nothing like mine, and she is quite mature for her age. I choose to learn from those whose lives are unlike mine in status, autonomy, in their roles. I could be friends with a Prince and just as friendly with a man who lives in a Ger in Mongolia. What is most fascinating though is I learn from them, and I realize that we, as humans, are more alike than we are different."*

Ron is a teacher in a special needs school. He surrounds himself with people who value his students. *"I welcome all my students into my life and I learn from them every day. Many have severe disabilities, but then so do I. They are no worse than I am. My students are my teachers.*

There's Joe, who has cerebral palsy and he taught me to smile. He taught me no matter what you can't do, there are things you can. He is 10 years old.

Then there's Jameel who is bipolar. Sometimes, he is filled with great happiness and joy. At other times, he is depressed and desperate. He continues to teach me how to live a good life. He once said to me, 'Sometimes you get a rotten apple, but you don't have to eat it. Choose another one. Life is for living with red, shiny apples.' Jameel focuses on those red, shiny apples more than I do. These are two of my teachers."

Their relations are based on trust and respect. Both teachers show resilient behavior. They are open and are able to learn from others. This is their message:

- Surround yourself with people you can learn from.
- Choose friends who support the person you are.
- Learn from people who are different from you.

DAILY PRACTICE

Today, in the staff room, say hello to a teacher whose skills you admire, although you don't know this colleague to well. What are his/her special skills? Observe him/her, spend time together and share your appreciation and your willingness to learn from him/her. Are you ready to step out of your comfort zone and learn from your fellow teacher's experience?

Reference to p. 124
Daily One Minute Meditation

DAY 48

SHOW COURAGE AND COMMITMENT

A resilient teacher will always show courage and commitment. Sometimes, your fear outweighs positive emotions and you will have to fight from within. It takes courage to achieve your vision and goals. It takes commitment to wake up every morning and make things happen.

Eli said, *"Pick up the pieces and think about the hurricane."* The hurricane didn't destroy him. The process wasn't fast, but he showed courage and determination. He used his experience to rebuild who he was as a person. This was his triumph boosted with courage and commitment.

Think about Betsy, a middle school science teacher, whose courage and commitment led her into a whole new world of discovery. *"I wanted to use interactive teaching methods in my classroom so my students would be more motivated. To this end, I signed up for an advanced teacher-training program. I walked into the training and found the participants were all experienced teachers who had graduated from the best universities and knew far more than I did about interactive teaching methods. The trainer's approach was very professional, following the curriculum for advanced level. Even though I was young and inexperienced, I attended the program to learn from the best. During the break, I wanted to connect with all these experienced teachers. I told one of them: 'I want to bring some fun in my teaching. Would you share with me your best practices?' She said I must first understand the theory. I went to another teacher who said more of the same. I didn't give up. I asked a third teacher at lunch and kept persisting until finally this teacher said, 'Yes, I will gladly share with you the most successful activities I've had with my students. I would also be interested in learning about the activities you have tried.' I kept in touch with this teacher and learned more and more from her. She became my mentor. Together, we wrote an innovative practical guide to introduce fun and interactive teaching techniques to the classroom."*

Betsy didn't give up. She had a vision, the courage, and the commitment to achieve her dream.

DAILY PRACTICE

Reflect on your vision and on one goal you want to achieve. Now think about three actions you need to take to accomplish your goal. How does courage and commitment match your vision and goals? On a scale on 1-5, measure your commitment and the courage it takes to carry out those three actions. Draw up an action plan and start with the one that has the highest score.

Reference to p. 124
Daily One Minute Meditation

DAY 49

BE ALWAYS AT THE TOP OF YOUR GAME!

This is a metaphor to guide you toward resilience. To stay at the top of your game is a skill that helps you be always at your best. A resilient teacher doesn't have to prove to himself or others that he is strong; he knows that failure and mistakes are part of life. A resilient teacher recognizes challenging situations may occur, yet he chooses to remain strong.

When you are at the top of your game, your behavior is similar to a successful athlete. You would certainly use the word resilience to define such an athlete. What do athletes and teachers have in common?

1. They work tirelessly to meet their goals.
2. They have a vision and the commitment to succeed.
3. They strengthen and fine-tune their skills
4. They have a positive attitude.
5. They trust their teams.
6. They are confident in themselves.
7. They strive to be the best.
8. They learn from and overcome their challenges.
9. They bounce forward.

10 They are mindful and resilient.

Just like an athlete, a teacher needs to perform in the classroom and be the best he/she can be, at all times. This is not always easy, but the skills you have learned can help you manage your stress and have a positive attitude at all times.

With consistent training, you can become a successful athlete in teaching. There is no difference between you and an athlete. The athlete plays with his/her team and the teacher works with the students in his/her class. The teacher's success is measured through the success of his/her students.

DAILY PRACTICE

Imagine you are an athlete, training for competition.

Visualize your successful team.

Acknowledge your emotions at your success.

Imagine you are in the classroom with your students, preparing for the exam.

Visualize your students' successful results.

Acknowledge your emotions at your success.

Reread the ten-point list; which trait laid the foundation for your success?

Reference to p. 124
Daily One Minute Meditation

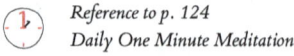

DAY 50

BUILD A MINDSET FOR BOUNCING FORWARD

Every day brings new challenges into your life. Some of these challenges will be easy to solve, while others may overwhelm you, building up stress and anxiety, lowering your motivation, enthusiasm and performance. During challenging times, resilience helps you deal with the situations you face. If your mindset is flexible and you are willing to learn from your mistakes, your difficulties become your teachers for further growth.

A flexible mindset will yield a wide range of positive results. For a bouncing-forward mindset, life's challenges are opportunities to grow. Obviously, on the other hand, a fixed mindset turns every problem into a hardship, missing the opportunities.

Dana, a dedicated history teacher, shared her experience with us: One day, she realized her mindset wasn't allowing her to perform the way she had hoped. *"I started every day with low energy, thinking ahead all the time about my students' low achievements, bad behavior, and my own exhausting hours. My mind was set for bad days and my students felt it."* One day, a colleague asked her: *"How are you, Dana?"* Dana surprised even herself with her answer: *"Don't even ask. My energy is so low and I can't even imagine that I still have the whole day ahead of me."* She didn't know why, but her quick reply haunted her for days. Then she realized, *"It's in my mind! It's the words I use that set the tone for the day. I've got to do something. I can't go on this way. I can start my day with awareness and intention. I can bounce forward whenever I feel like hardships are pushing on my shoulders."* This decision changed her mood and her way of thinking. She chose to look at *good days* instead of *bad days*. When she changed her mindset to *good days*, she found she had positive energy. Her new mindset impacted her students and her colleagues. Dana knew that bad things might still happen, but as her mind was set for *good days*, her new way of thinking became positive.

Dana teaches us how resilience changed her power. She could have stayed on the same path, living a fixed mindset. She decided to use her skills and her own power to bounce forward to serve her and her students.

Eli's story taught us that, no matter what happens in your life, you have the power within to go on and "build a better version of yourself." He shared what resilience meant for him and how he could rebuild himself by using his mindset to bounce forward. With his teacher's support, he gained the power to accept and let go of his past so that he could move on.

We don't have to be attached to our pains and our disappointments. We can learn to let them go and move forward. Take small steps. Some may be part of your everyday life, while others may need more work. Take a deep breath and give yourself permission to move forward.

DAILY PRACTICE

Think about your vision, goals and skills as a resilient teacher. To bounce forward you need to know your vision and goals as a resilient teacher. Let's take a scale from one to five, where one is the lowers and five is the highest level for your skills. Place an x along the line below the number where you believe you are right now.

Answer the following questions:

Have you got the commitment to achieve your goals?

1 2 3 4 5

Can you forgive yourself and others?

1 2 3 4 5

Can you bounce forward?

1 2 3 4 5

What can you do to move up along the line?

Reference to p. 124
Daily One Minute Meditation

CHAPTER 6

THE CONSCIOUS CLASSROOM

We live in a world that emphasizes professional achievements. Working in a friendly, warm, and stimulating environment will help you truly succeed in the teaching profession. A mindful and resilient teacher needs to teach beyond mere academics. This chapter expands the awareness of your teaching experience and helps you use your wisdom to create a conscious classroom - a class with a heart, where the teacher is aware of the students' needs and is mindfully present to fulfill them.

Your presence cannot be separated from the context of the classroom. It supports your principles and the way you act. Therefore, you need to pay attention to the entire classroom environment: the daily messages you communicate to your students, your management skills, while keeping the room clean, visually pleasing, and uncluttered. All these factors enhance learning and reduce stress, creating a serene teaching environment.

As you create such an environment, you role-model positive behavior, and your actions are likely to help you achieve your vision. We have created ten such actions for the next ten days. You have successfully covered the first 50 days, half of your journey.

Day 51. Make an Impact
Day 52. Build Conscious Relationships
Day 53. Role-model Positive Behavior
Day 54. Reconnect with Yourself
Day 55. Pay Attention to Your Senses
Day 56. Create a Conscious Classroom Environment
Day 57. Manage Your Time Wisely
Day 58. Form Purposeful Routines
Day 59. Pause in Silence and Look Inward
Day 60. Acknowledge the Strengths of Your Students

DAY 51

MAKE AN IMPACT

In Chapters Four and Five, *The Mindful Teacher* and *The Resilient Teacher*, you explored ways to become mindful and resilient, so that you may start building your conscious classroom. It is a classroom based on healthy relationships between you and your students, and among your students, supported by well-established routines and by the experience you've shared with your students. The conscious classroom is a nurturing environment that helps you and your students overcome challenging situations. Your vision plays an important role in your efforts to create such an environment. You will reflect about this environment to make sure it has a profound impact and it will make a difference in your students' lives.

When Dr. Evans, a high school English teacher, realized his students were losing interest in his class, he started to reflect on his vision about teaching. He knew he mastered the subject matter and he could use his expertise to reach his goals and get positive results in this teaching practice. However, he felt something was missing. He started to search for answers and realized that, to reach his goals, he needed to focus on interpersonal relationships. He met Susan at a workshop, and they talked about best practices in teaching. Susan emphasized the importance of becoming mindful of himself and of his students' needs. Dr. Evans made a pledge to himself, *"I am committed to bring enthusiasm and motivation in all my classes, beyond the academics, and I know it only depends on me."*

He took the first step toward creating a conscious classroom: he greeted his students with enthusiasm every day. He continued to adjust his teaching approach and kept a list of those changes that had a real impact on his teaching:

1. *I greet my students with enthusiasm every time I enter the classroom.*
2. *I smile and make jokes when I feel tension in class in order to lighten the atmosphere.*
3. *I share interesting facts with my students, and I listen to their stories.*
4. *I encourage them and give them feedback on their work and behavior.*

Dr. Evans managed to bring enthusiasm and motivation to his classroom. He also built and kept a good relationship with his students throughout the year. He became aware of his students' needs and offered them the support they needed. He gave them his undivided attention, opened the door to their hearts, and kept the spark in their eyes alive.

DAILY PRACTICE

For one day, imagine you are your own shadow. Follow yourself throughout the day from the moment you arrive at school. Observe how you enter your classroom, how present you are for your students during class, and how your relationship with them looks through the eyes of an observer. At the end of the day, make a list of suggestions to create enthusiasm and motivation in the classroom. You may look at Dr. Evans's list and make small improvements; no more than one small action every day.

ONE MINUTE MEDITATION FOR CHAPTER 6

Find a comfortable seated position.

Close your eyes or lower your gaze.

Rest your hands in your lap, palms up.

Bring your awareness to your breath.

Inhale through your nose for 4 counts.

Exhale through your mouth for 6 counts.

Place your hand on your heart.

Feel its beat.

Imagine your classroom.

Think of all you give your students by being present in their learning and growth.

Appreciate the energy you bring to the room.

Your presence in the *here* and *now* makes a difference.

Return to your breath.

Inhale through your nose for 4 counts.

Exhale through your mouth for 6 counts.

Smile as you slowly open your eyes!

DAY 52

BUILD CONSCIOUS RELATIONSHIPS

Give your students wings to fly and they will. Such action demonstrates the thinking pattern of a mindful and resilient teacher, who will create the unique environment of a conscious classroom. In a conscious classroom, students can learn with confidence, find the courage to spread their wings, and fly.

A conscious classroom means that your students have personal choice, and you teach them to be accountable for their decisions. They are passionate about learning because you encourage them to express their thoughts, concerns, and opinions. You help them understand who they are. You have to ensure clear and effective communication with your students. A good starting point could be to understand their generation. You need to know how they learn because it is different from how you learned. You did not have access to technology as they do. They did not experience the same history as you did. Their generation tells you something about who they are and how you should teach them. Differences between generations have always existed! Who hasn't said to their parents, *"You just don't understand!"*

Recognize that you and your students have different points of view, upbringing, history, and perceptions. These are all qualities that make your generation unique to you and your students' generation unique to theirs. However, as their teacher, it is your responsibility to reach out and understand them.

Relationships between generations are built with empathy and compassion, not with lecturing and the arrogance of the 'older and wiser'. Note that teaching is not just about talking, it is also about listening. The way you listen and talk to your students creates the framework for the bond between student and educator.

After you get to know your students, practice deep listening. Keep your attention on what they say and control the impulse to judge and criticize them. Show an honest curiosity and try to understand their needs. When you practice deep listening, you also teach them how to become good listeners.

When you speak to them, use mindful talk. Make sure they understand what you mean and they won't misinterpret your words. Be open to their comments and don't take them personally. Your words are very important; choose them carefully. Build a positive vocabulary, using a warm and encouraging tone of voice so their trust can grow and their wings get ready to fly.

DAILY PRACTICE

A conscious classroom is built on trust and open relationships. Reflect on how you can overcome the difficulties arising from the generation gap between you and your students. Change starts with awareness.

Reflect on the following questions:

How aware are you of the differences between you and your students today?

Share with them your observations and invite them to tell you their expectations and ideas for learning.

Listen to them without judgement and try not to take it personally. Act instead of react.

How can you meet their expectations?

Choose one thing you can learn from them and follow it through.

Reference to p. 152
Daily One Minute Meditation

DAY 53

ROLE MODEL POSITIVE BEHAVIOR

The term role model generally refers to a person who serves as an example and whose behavior is emulated by others. We usually think of a role model as someone other than ourselves. It could be a president, a charismatic TV personality, or a person with tremendous wisdom.

As you create a new model of teaching, your mental shift is the recognition that you can be a role model. Your students absorb information and learn at a rapid pace, and you are their example. What you do, what you say, and how you feel about them will come through in their behavior. This is your legacy.

What makes you a role model? When you are mindful and show resilience, you have a positive impact on your students. You listen deeply, engage in mindful conversations with them, and work towards positive outcomes. You teach them courage and determination through your actions and help them reach their full potential. By choosing teaching as a profession, you have chosen to become a role model to your students. So, how do you become the best role model you can be?

Your students automatically observe what you do. They listen to your words when you speak, notice your body language, and sense your mood. Your attitude is what they will remember. Therefore:

1. If you are offended by a student's behavior, reflect on his/her behavior and don't use harsh words in return.

2. If a student belittles another student, make sure you do not belittle the first student when you reprimand him/her.

3. If you are offended by a student, be aware you will not regain your power by admonishing him/her; practice empathy and compassion at all times.

4. If you are frustrated when a colleague uses bad language in the staff room, make sure you reject that language and do not use it at any time.

Keep in mind that your students learn from your behavior, and you teach them simply by walking into the classroom every day.

DAILY PRACTICE

Think back to your school days. You were once young like your students, and you had role models who helped you shape into the person you are today. Some may have contributed to your successes, while others may have contributed to issues you face because of their behavior. What can you learn from your past?

Think about what you believe is most important to share with your students. Imagine they are grown-ups, working in today's society to benefit others. Most likely, they will embrace the values and beliefs you hold true. How can you make sure you role model the features you want them to emulate?

Reference to p. 152
Daily One Minute Meditation

DAY 54

RECONNECT WITH YOURSELF

You have the special responsibility to impart higher values to your students and to make sure their academic skills are at the grade level. You face challenges today that didn't exist years ago. Times are different. One can't live an insular life; we are all connected. It can be beautiful and, at the same time, it can be overwhelming.

While we researched this book, we observed classrooms around the world, spoke with teachers of all subject matters and grades, and tried to find the common thread that fosters effective teaching and learning.

We realized that teachers who draw from their strengths within can reconnect with themselves and can easily overcome daily challenges. When you teach with confidence and integrity, students will emulate your behavior. Schools are more and more interested in supporting the well-being of teachers and students.

Different programs have been implemented around the world to support teachers in their efforts to achieve the peace of mind they need, so they can teach with enthusiasm and passion. Such programs include training, workshops, and mentoring modules, along with initiatives to change and adapt the school environment to meet teachers' needs. This may include, besides trainings, seminars, and mentoring programs, mentoring modules, along with initiatives to remodeling and adapting the school environment to meet all these needs.

The first step in the Well-being Program of Transylvania College, Romania, was to create the *Mindfulness Room*, a shared meeting room where teachers and students will engage in mindful and meaningful conversations. The second step took the teachers' well-being issues further by designing a *Silent Room* where the faculty can spend quiet time to restore their energy. The *Silent Room* is furnished with couches, cushions, and floor rugs and has become a highly appreciated place. Adding these two specially designed rooms to the usual school environment considerably improved the overall atmosphere and the quality of teaching.

Every school will come up with different solutions. Whatever the situation, teachers are often on auto-pilot running from class to class, planning, and preparing. Allow yourself to stop and reconnect with yourself during the day, to lower the stress, become mindful and resilient, so you can better guide and inspire your students during each class you teach.

DAILY PRACTICE

Create a silent place in your mind. Make it a place where you imagine you can take a few minutes to be alone with your thoughts and emotions. You can imagine that you are in this place when you look out of the window, take a short walk outside, or when you enjoy a cup of tea or coffee in silence. You can always create your own silent place. Acknowledge the need to recharge your batteries and pause in silence.

Reference to p. 152
Daily One Minute Meditation

DAY 55

PAY ATTENTION TO YOUR SENSES

You embraced the journey to become a mindful and resilient teacher, and you are now on the steady path to become aware not only of your thoughts and emotions but also of the physical surroundings in the classroom. Everything starts with you. Your awareness is the starting point to create the warm and friendly learning environment of the *conscious classroom,* as we call it in this book. How often do you pay attention to your senses? Everyone is influenced by light, sounds, and the smell of fresh air. All these factors affect the quality of teaching.

Light: Lighting plays an important role in your classroom. Be aware of natural and artificial lighting in your surroundings and use them as needed. Notice which type of light appeals to your students and make the most of it. It affects the way they see you and the information you present. It helps them concentrate and achieve their best results. Lack of light can make them tired and too much light can hurt their eyes.

Sounds: The noise level can impact teaching and learning. An increased level of noise in a classroom becomes distracting. Awareness of the sounds around you helps you find strategies to lower the noise and create an active listening environment.

Air: The lack of fresh air leads to fatigue and lack of concentration. You can provide a better environment, where teaching and learning improve, by simply opening the windows or doors.

We realized that awareness of the environment can help and support you and your students. When you live in the present, you acknowledge your surroundings, you look for solutions, and you interact with your students in a beneficial way. As you have already learned, breathing exercises will help you remain centered and find greater clarity of yourself and of the surrounding environment.

DAILY PRACTICE

Enter your classroom and pay attention to your senses. What is the first thing you notice? Is it the light, the sounds or the smells?

Share your observations with your students and explain to them how this affects their learning. Make up a list of actions you can take in order to create a better learning environment - a conscious classroom.

Reference to p. 152
Daily One Minute Meditation

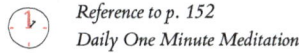

DAY 56

CREATE A CONSCIOUS CLASSROOM ENVIRONMENT

The classroom is not only a place to teach but also a place where you bring the miracle of learning. How can you create and maintain this miracle? Your journey as a mindful and resilient teacher enhances the awareness of your teaching. Every time you enter your classroom, you observe things you like and things you'd prefer not to have around. Your students feel the same.

We spoke about the importance of light, sound, and smells in the classroom. A conscious classroom also encourages students to practice cooperative and individual learning. Your classroom can have special areas designed for working in groups, as well as a quiet corner for solitary work. Make sure your furniture is arranged in a way that offers your students opportunities to work both ways. Whether you teach elementary school or high school, whether you have your own classroom or you share it with another colleague, your students will benefit from working both in teams and individually.

You need to pay attention to the furniture setup. A room has walls, doors, and windows, which can all be used creatively, so that they turn your classroom into a stimulating and joyful environment. Work done by students can be displayed alongside positive messages, rules, and useful information. Make their work attractive and colorful to catch the eye of the observer. Use music during a lesson to lower the stress and calm your students' minds.

Laura, a middle-school Romanian teacher, was concerned because her students weren't focused, and she couldn't achieve the results she wished for. One day, she asked her colleagues to come to her classroom and sit in her students' seats. She became a student too and asked one of her colleagues to teach the class. She said, *"During the time spent as a student, I realized it was hard to stay focused for such a long time while sitting at a desk in the third row. When the teacher told me to focus on the text, my mind wandered elsewhere. I realized that I had lost my focus and my mind was wandering. Then, I imagined myself being back home, sitting on the couch, reading the text I had in front of me. At the end of the lesson, I asked my colleagues how they felt as students, and if they had any ideas to share to improve the learning experience. Many ideas have been debated, but my idea got the highest number of votes: the need to create a warm and cozy space in the classroom for the students. During the next few days, my students brought bean-bags, pillows and a small carpet, created a cozy place and named it Mindful Corner – a place to relax, focus, and enjoy a good book."*

DAILY PRACTICE

Sit silently for one minute. Take time to reconnect with yourself and pause. Take three deep breaths and become aware of your classroom environment. Imagine yourself as a student in your own classroom. Put yourself in their shoes and be aware of the things you can change to meet your needs as a learner. Do this exercise with your students. Ask them what they would change to enhance their learning experience. Make a list of their needs and choose one to fulfill within a month - the one that has the deepest impact on you all.

Reference to p. 152
Daily One Minute Meditation

DAY 57

MANAGE YOUR TIME WISELY

There are things you need to do and things you want to do. Whatever the case, when you focus on too many things at the same time, you feel pressure and frustration, blaming everything on the lack of time. Every day, you make decisions concerning your time. You might often find yourself automatically using the phrase: *"I don't have time to ..."*

You own your time. How do you manage it? When you use it wisely, you model this behavior to your students. So, think carefully about your relationship with time. Figure out how you can best teach them to use their time wisely. Demonstrate you are not controlled by the clock on the wall, but by respect and responsibilities for yourself and others. Talk with your students about actions that show respect and responsibility. *"I am in class on time every day. I maximize my teaching time. I make sure I spend time to show each of you that I care about you."* Actions speak louder than words, but repeating the words to them does reinforce your intentional behavior. *"I make sure I keep my promises to each and every one of you. Please let me know if I don't follow through."*

Lack of time is a major stress inducer. When you are running out of time, your mind loses focus, and you feel overwhelmed. When you are stressed over time, your students feel it. You have a budget of 24 hours a day, and you have to spend this amount of time wisely to keep your classroom warm and relaxed. Become a better time manager so you can enjoy a relaxed and mindful atmosphere in your classroom.

Even though time and mindfulness may sound like different concepts, they coexist. Time is concrete and sequential. You are bound to follow a time schedule, which shows resilience. You are prepared, organized, and committed to meet certain goals. Mindfulness is an abstract concept. It is a state of mind, something less tangible than a time schedule. However, mindfulness is equally important to you as a teacher. When you are overwhelmed and time is compressed, you lose control over the atmosphere within the classroom. Focus on your breath and live in the present moment. When you breathe slowly, time expands. This can also be called timefulness.

Follow these time suggestions:

- Do you want your students to value time? Help them out.
- Do you want your students to take time for themselves? Teach them how.
- Do you want to offer your students a sense of peace? Follow a calm path.

Time is a precious thing you own. It is a gift you can offer in all kinds of situations: when you give your full attention to a student, when you manage it wisely for the benefit of others.

Annie, a kindergarten teacher, shared with us her experience. "*I felt exhausted all the time. My teaching hours were long. I couldn't get my work done. My family needed me, but I found it difficult to meet their expectations. It was hard to be a good teacher, a good mother, and still find time to take care of myself! I felt I was missing out on many things in my life!*"

When she realized she couldn't go on like that any longer, Annie decided to change her situation. She decided to become a better time manager with a budget of 24 hours daily. She thought about the way she was spending her time and started to prioritize her activities, assigning a certain amount of time for each item. This included teaching hours, preparation hours, time spent with students, and time spent with her friends and family.

Annie created her own mindful clock, including all these activities. The mindful clock helped Annie be more organized and mindful and had beneficial effects on her overall well-being.

Mindful clock – Manage Your Time Wisely

DAILY PRACTICE

How do you manage your time during the school day? Make a list with the time allocated to the various activities. Create your mindful clock and make sure you allow time to get the important things done. Never forget to set aside time for yourself every day. Remember to take a pause when you are stressed and get back to your breathing. Focusing on your breath and living in the present moment will help you gain control of your life. When you are stressed out, time feels compressed.

Reference to p. 152
Daily One Minute Meditation

DAY 58

FORM PURPOSEFUL ROUTINES

Routines are rhythmic patterns that create a safe and predictable environment to further develop healthy habits. As we have mentioned before, time is a very valuable resource. To make the most of your available time, routines help you focus on the goals of the lesson you teach and put distractions aside.

Routines can help you design a conscious classroom and give you structure to fulfill your goals. Don't try to get into too many routines at the same time, but be conscious of them and go over them regularly. Routines need to be clear and specific, reinforced through repetition. Show your students the behavior you expect. Describe the importance of the routine with kindness and consistency.

Michaela, an elementary school teacher, was unhappy with her noisy class. She had to stop often to get her students' attention. She knew she had to do something differently to change the situation. She decided to speak openly with them about this issue and, together, they came up with the idea to assign a "noise level coordinator." The coordinator had an orange card on his/her desk. Every time the noise level went over the limit, the coordinator would put up the orange card, while saying: *"Only one person speaks at a time!"* If the noise level didn't get lower, the teacher would step in and say, *"Stop and breathe!"* A new coordinator would be assigned every six weeks. The first coordinator who volunteered was the student who kept interrupting most frequently.

Michaela addressed the disruptions constructively and created a routine to manage the noise level and to restore focus and pleasant atmosphere in the classroom. It takes time and patience to implement routines. Don't give up; be mindful and resilient. It will work both for you and for your students' benefit.

DAILY PRACTICE

Reflect on the following questions to create your own set of classroom routines.

1. Which are those moments in your class that could be improved by a set of well defined routines?

2. Do you consider implementing time for reflection or meditation in your class as routines for improvement?

Talk with your students about the importance of routines, including reflection or meditation.

Reference to p. 152
Daily One Minute Meditation

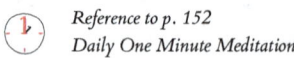

DAY 59

PAUSE IN SILENCE AND LOOK INWARD

The increased amount of information in the 21st century affects all of us both in a positive and a negative way. Stress develops mostly due to the daily pressure. Stress can impede the learning process and affect the students' mental and physical well-being. The number of students on antidepressants has increased dramatically all around the globe. Millions suffer from learning disorders. Youth suicide rate also grows at a rapid pace.

A mindful and resilient teacher in the 21st century is aware of all these dangers and recognizes the need to create an improved classroom environment for the students where their development is safe, healthy, and happy. There are various procedures to help create a healthy learning environment. If your students are stressed, it affects you too.

Let's consider one procedure to make it easier for you to create a conscious classroom for the benefit of your students. A silent pause is an opportunity to create serenity. This simple practice can be beneficial for all of us. We suggest that you take a 15-second pause in silence at the beginning of the class or anytime during the school day when you find chaos or disorder in the classroom. Set up a routine to make it easier to implement it. Even though it is for a very short period of time, it highlights the concept of silence. You may talk with your students about the positive effects they feel after this 15 second pause. The pause can be increased to one minute, if necessary.

DAILY PRACTICE

Take a pause to bring silence to your classroom today. Use this pause when your students are fidgety or unfocused. They may wonder how this silent pause benefits them. Explain the benefits to them; make them stop and pause for 15 seconds while they reconnect with themselves. Call this time *Pause in Silence* and reflect on how it makes them feel.

Reference to p. 152
Daily One Minute Meditation

DAY 60

ACKNOWLEDGE THE STRENGTHS OF YOUR STUDENTS

On Level Three – *Actions*, you identified and practiced ways to become a mindful and resilient teacher who can create a conscious classroom, a stimulating environment for teaching. Your presence, attitude, and your behavior support your teaching.

Be always aware of your thoughts, emotions and words. Your attitude and behavior guide your students in their learning journey. Each student has strengths you may or may not see. All of them are special; just look for the genius in each one of them!

Picture yourself in your classroom during one of your classes. It doesn't matter whether it is science, math, or reading. Just imagine you are standing in front of your students, teaching your class. Listed below are your students; they are just children at this time, not famous personalities yet:

- Albert Einstein
- Pablo Picasso
- Lionel Messi
- Michael Jackson
- J. K. Rowling
- Ludwig Van Beethoven
- Michael Jordan

How would you tailor your lesson for each of them?

Now, think about your students. How will they turn out?

The teachers who taught the students above didn't know how they would turn out. Your students may surprise you too. Teach each of them as if they are all geniuses and always remember to look for their spark!

DAILY PRACTICE

Challenge yourself as a teacher to look at your students and find everyone's strengths. Give special attention to the students who interrupt most of the time and don't usually focus in your class. Look at your students from a different perspective, building on their strengths. Give them feedback and make them aware of what they are good at. To check that you are teaching at the right pace, look at your students' eyes, see if they shine and teach in a way that keeps their spark alive.

Notes

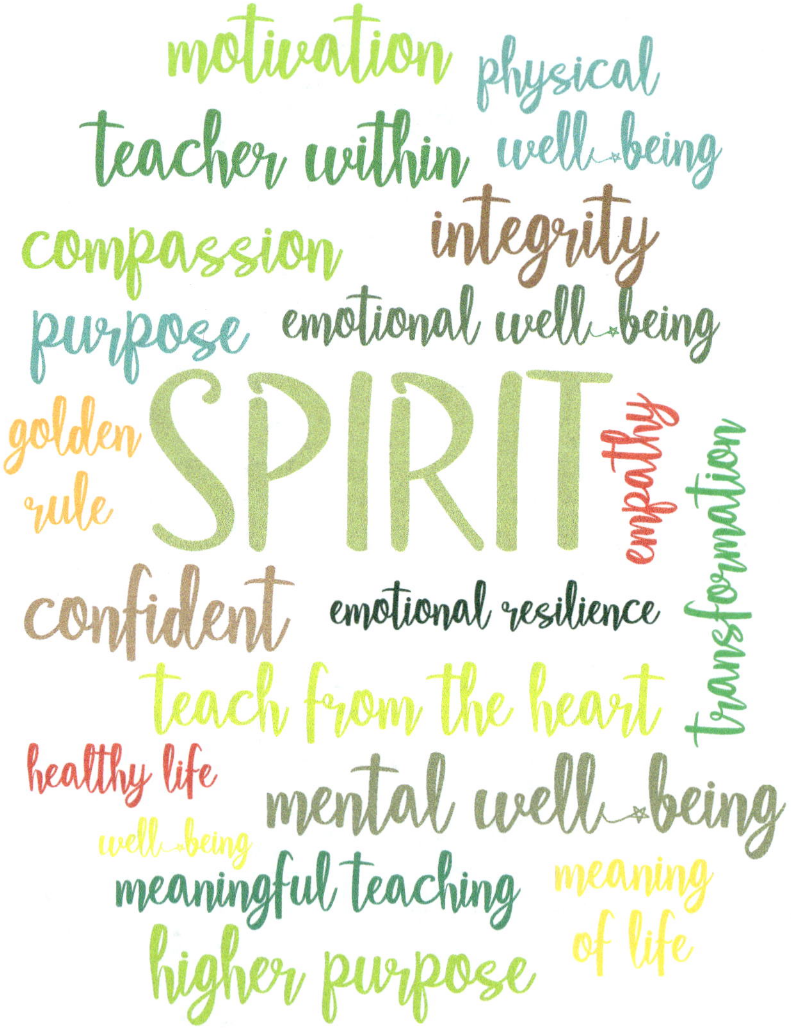
motivation
physical
teacher within
well-being
integrity
compassion
purpose
emotional well-being
SPIRIT
golden rule
empathy
transformation
confident
emotional resilience
teach from the heart
healthy life
mental well-being
well-being
meaningful teaching
meaning of life
higher purpose

LEVEL FOUR

TRANSFORMATION

transformation

CHAPTER 7

EMOTIONAL WELL-BEING

In this chapter, we quote the motto, *mens sana in corpore sano* – a healthy mind in a healthy body. Let's use this motto as we focus on the importance of a healthy mind that has the ability to be aware and control thoughts, emotions, and actions. All of us want to live a healthy and happy life.

Throughout the book, you have so far learned about the importance of increasing your awareness, of recognizing your thoughts, and of addressing your emotions through your core concerns. Through the *Daily Practices* and *One Minute Meditations* you took specific actions to become mindful and resilient. Take the next ten days and use these emotions as your guide. You will be your own teacher – learn about your emotions! These lessons help you acknowledge and accept your emotions, both positive and negative, such as love, anger, trust, frustration, respect, kindness, and self-compassion.

Positive emotions will have an impact on your health; emotions are directly connected to your body. When you experience love, your heartbeat is different, hands get sweatier, you may laugh or even cry easier. Anger can make you feel sick and give you headaches or insomnia. Emotions influence your immune system, your memory; you can't ignore them, nor can you suppress them.

Emotions affect your thinking as well. If you are angry, your head gets filled with negative emotions, you walk in the classroom bad-tempered, and you let your emotions affect your teaching. Your emotions affect you as well as your students and their learning process.

Emotions affect your behavior. If you don't know how to control your emotions, you may raise your voice at your students in case of a conflict. However, when you become aware of your emotions, you will be able to choose the way you respond; you will be thinking proactively rather than reactively. You will listen to your students mindfully and manage your emotions effectively.

You recognize the need to pause, breathe, and focus in order to understand the person you are talking to. Your mind generates thoughts all the time.

In Chapter 7, you will get a deeper understanding of your emotions and how they can serve you. Over the next ten days, you follow the path of emotional well-being.

Day 61. Welcome Your Emotions
Day 62. Show Acts of Love
Day 63. Give and Receive Acts of Kindness
Day 64. Embrace Forgiveness
Day 65. Bring Compassion into Your Life
Day 66. Witness Your Fears
Day 67. Be Confident in Yourself
Day 68. Build Emotional Resilience
Day 69. Be Aware of Your Concerns
Day 70. Teach from Your Heart

DAY 61

WELCOME YOUR EMOTIONS

Your emotions are like the weather. You will have rainy days and sunny days. Both are part of your life. Positive and negative emotions will always be there and, if you recognize and embrace them, you can make the best of them. Negative emotions do not have to dominate your life and they may even contribute to it. Just think about how fear helps you create better rules and safety systems. You are not afraid when you cross the road, because you have rules that protect you; you are not afraid to dive into the swimming pool, because you know the depth of the pool and you have your own rules that work for you.

If you don't know how to manage your negative emotions, you allow blame and judgment dominate your mind. You may become attached to old stories which hurt you in the past and come back to haunt you over and over again. If you become aware of these attachments, you can choose to release them and empower yourself to treat your pain and anger with kindness.

We are not saying that you have to be always happy; you can feel in different ways and still find the inner strength to deal with negative emotions. When you think negative thoughts, accept them and try to learn from them. In time, they will no longer have power over you. They will be like the weather; you will always have rainy days and sunny days.

Each of us has an amazing collection of positive and negative thoughts. Every student, teacher, and administrator you see has both kinds of thoughts and emotions. Many of our negative thoughts are justified. For example, if you hear an unusual sound in your house at night, you automatically generate a negative thought and emotion such as worry or fear. Emotions are generated to protect and guide us. You may think it's a burglar, a ghost, or something fearful. It takes a while to switch your mind to positive thinking and say: *it's just the wind*. It depends on you not to empower the negative thought and create a scenario that supports it. When you let go of negative thoughts, you can regain your peace of mind, welcome positive thoughts, and generate positive emotions. Learn to embrace both the negative and positive emotions, but don't get attached to the negative ones.

DAILY PRACTICE

Reflect on your emotions and pay attention to the message they send. Do not judge or blame them. "What is the lesson I have learned from this experience?"

Look at your emotions as you embrace them and ask yourself: "How can I grow from this?"

Teach your students how can they embrace their emotions and learn from them.

ONE MINUTE MEDITATION FOR CHAPTER 7

Find a comfortable seated position.

Close your eyes or lower your gaze.

Rest your hands in your lap, palms up.

Bring your awareness to your breath.

Inhale through your nose for 4 counts.

Exhale through your mouth for 6 counts.

Think of a situation when you were harsh on yourself.

Reverse the situation, be kind and appreciate yourself.

Fill your heart with understanding.

Accept your feelings and notice how your body reacts.

Take one deep breath.

Inhale through your nose for 4 counts.

Exhale through your mouth for 6 counts.

Compassion begins in yourself.

Smile as you slowly open your eyes!

DAY 62

SHOW ACTS OF LOVE

Defining love could be an almost impossible task. It is a feeling you find within yourself and an act you do toward others. Love helps you overcome fears and empowers you when things get tough. It is a means of understanding what is most important for you in life; what is ideal and what you seek. Love ultimately holds all of us together and gives meaning to our lives. In its foundation, all our wishes go back to the need for love.

In your classroom, a loving and caring environment reflects the way you act and manage the class under any circumstances. As one of the teachers at the Sandy Hook Elementary School in Newtown, Connecticut, said, when her classroom was under gunfire, *"Hide, dear children, here in the bathroom, with me. I love you all more than anything else on earth. You are my reason for living. You are all going to be okay."*

In times of crisis, we often find what is most important to us. But we don't have to wait for something extreme to happen. Every second we show love to our students builds their trust.

As a teacher, you spend most of your time with your students in the classroom. If you want your students to spread love in their lives, it is your role to model such behavior through your teaching. A teacher who cares for his/her students will always take extra steps to make them feel safe, accepted, and listened to.

Sometimes, you see students hurt themselves or others, demanding extra attention. You don't know why this is happening. In order to understand it, you'll have to look at the entire picture. These children are not only part of a classroom; they are highly affected by their home environment, as well as by their community. Your responsibility, though, is to be loving and kind to all students, bearing in mind that their behavior is connected to both school and home. By watching them and understanding their needs and circumstances, we can fill their bucket of love with special attention and care.

What the teacher from Sandy Hook Elementary did by protecting the children under attack was a proof of love and care for them in school, so they could go home safely.

DAILY PRACTICE

No matter the age of your students or the subject you teach, bring love and care in each class.

Create a box in your classroom where students can share the way they experience love and care, both at school and home. Encourage them to write notes, letters, or bring photos of loved ones. Learn more about their life outside of school to understand them better and become the support they need.

Reference to p. 180
Daily One Minute Meditation

DAY 63

GIVE AND RECEIVE ACTS OF KINDNESS

Let's continue our journey toward emotional well-being. Allow yourself to bring kindness into your life, which is love in its pure essence. It is like a band-aid for your heart, mind, and body. Our world can be a better place if we could just learn to show kindness to others.

We study many subjects in school, and we receive all kinds of useful information; however, we never learn about kindness, generosity, or gratefulness. Kindness doesn't need to be a separate subject; it can be integrated in every aspect of your teaching. Acts of kindness will show appreciation to your students, will make them happy, and you will feel the same.

We often say: *"the more you give, the more you receive."* This statement is valid for acts of kindness. When you are spontaneously kind to someone, you benefit as well. Whenever you perform an act of kindness, you give a piece of yourself to someone else. You may consider acts of kindness like the water that hydrates your body, creating a sensation of well-being. Acts of kindness are inexhaustible, from simple thoughts and words to actions; they bring beauty into your life. Kindness changes the way you think and it adds value and happiness to your life.

You can lower the bullying rate and reach your students' hearts by creating a culture of acts of kindness in schools. Fill your students' emotional tanks with encouragement, words of appreciation, and smiles.

Karin, a third-grade teacher, created a board called *Acts of Kindness* in her classroom. The motto on the board was: *Be Kind. Bring Smiles.* Karin encouraged everyone, teachers and students alike, to do acts of kindness both in school and at home and share them on the board. At the end of the month, the class voted for the kindest person, based on the actions they all took and posted on the board. The first month's winner was Sally. She sent daily *thank you* notes to the people in school who were never noticed by others: janitors, gatekeepers, and kitchen personnel. Sally's act of kindness inspired her classmates and her teachers. They all followed her example for the rest of the year.

DAILY PRACTICE

Make a list with all your students, colleagues, and maintenance personnel. Learn their names by heart and address them by their name each time you speak to them. They will feel valued and appreciated. Every person matters!

Reference to p. 180
Daily One Minute Meditation

DAY 64

EMBRACE FORGIVENESS

When you are open to love and kindness, you bring forgiveness into your life. Forgiveness allows you to release negative emotions and strengthen your emotional well-being. Forgiveness is more than simply saying *"I forgive you."* It helps you release your pain. Instead of focusing on the pain, allow forgiveness to enter your thoughts.

Forgiveness involves your ego, the part of your brain dealing with your self-esteem and self-importance. Forgiveness begins with your thoughts and moves to your emotions. It becomes an action when you change your behavior. You expand the wisdom inside you, raising it to a higher level of awareness.

At this moment, let's assume you are angry with someone close to you. Close your eyes and feel the anger in your mind. Imagine this anger is taking control of you. It grabs you and takes over your life. Your whole brain is consumed with this anger. Anger becomes who you are and your single goal is retribution. You want to take revenge on that person. You hate others because you are angry. Anger becomes your shadow, and you wake up in the morning starting the day with it.

Now, let's shift the mindset. At this moment, allow love to enter your life. It becomes your goal and your mind is filled with love and forgiveness. It adds to every part of your life. You smile at others and welcome your positive emotions. The love and forgiveness within you help you empathize with others. Love is your shadow and you wake up in the morning starting the day with it.

What changed in these two situations? You! Love entered the second scenario, making room for forgiveness. No one has to change, but you. It doesn't matter whom you must forgive, including yourself; it is your mindset you need to change.

A story from Rose, an educational consultant: *"I had a difficult childhood because my father was emotionally abusive, never accepting my ideas and my choices. He would never approve anything I did. I don't like to think of those times that had such a negative impact on me. I felt anger and frustration all the time. I carried those feelings until our son, Dan, was born. The first time I held him, I looked at his tiny face and said, "I will be a good mother to you. I will love you and support you all my life." In time, I learned to forgive my father, who died several years ago. I also realized that I have a choice of what kind of parent I wanted to become for my son. I looked up at the sky and said to my father, "I forgive you. I release my anger and welcome the joy of motherhood."*

What motivates you to forgive and what will replace the emptiness created after forgiveness? It's the love shown to yourself and others. Some people call this a healing process. We like to call it "the way to achieve emotional well-being." Forgiveness will help you release the pain you feel deep down in your heart and the negative emotions connected to pain. When you forgive, you create the foundation for healthy relationships.

Onion – Embrace Forgiveness

Some people say it is easier to forgive others than it is to forgive ourselves. We don't know the absolute truth, but the process of forgiveness, though difficult, has a beneficial effect on our mental health. So, when you catch yourself with a negative thought about you or others, recognize it and say to yourself, *"I am sorry. Please forgive me."* Focus on feeling good, be your own friend and stop hurting yourself. Treat yourself with love and gratitude, do good things which bring you pleasure and fill your emotional tank every day.

DAILY PRACTICE

Explain to your students about forgiveness:

"Forgiveness is like peeling an onion. When you peel the onion, you take off layer by layer and it might make you teary. Forgiveness is a process that could also bring tears to your eyes. However, you slowly go through the layers, and the closer you get to the essence, the better you will feel in both cases. Forgiveness can be hard, but then, when you wipe your tears away, you will be able to see things more clearly and put your smile back on your face. You will feel relieved and content."

Reference to p. 180
Daily One Minute Meditation

DAY 65

BRING COMPASSION INTO YOUR LIFE

When you accept and embrace forgiveness, you bring compassion into your life. You recognize your own needs, you can connect with and become empathetic with others. This can be a support for you throughout your day. The teaching profession is challenging and demanding, and teachers sometimes face what we call "teacher burnout." The source of burnout is often the process of thinking too many negative thoughts. It happens often, especially at those times when you cannot work efficiently in class and you cannot manage your students. How do you move from this pattern of negative emotions to positive ones?

When you are aware of your inner voice, you can start to practice self-compassion, sending kind thoughts to yourself. Talk to yourself the way you would talk to your best friend. Use a friendly tone and appreciate what you have. Acknowledge that, even if you don't have the best day, you can still do the best for yourself.

Compassion means you have the power within to care for yourself and others with kindness and empathy. When you include compassion in your life, you decrease your stress levels, you become healthier and happier. Compassion helps you feel what others feel, so you can find new perspectives easier. It is said "it takes a village to raise a child." Paraphrasing this, we can say "it takes a village to raise yourself." Compassion creates a climate of love, peace, and caring in your village. Alongside compassion, self-compassion enhances your well-being and helps you bounce forward whenever you face challenges!

Mindfulness, conscious breathing, and meditation may help you return to the present moment and release the negative emotions to make place for love, kindness, and forgiveness.

A pause, a moment of silence during the day may reconnect you with yourself, giving you the self-confidence you need to overcome challenges.

DAILY PRACTICE

Let's start with the assumption that you need "to build your village to rise yourself." Reflect on how you could enhance your well-being through compassion. Write three self-talk affirmations you can use when you face difficult times.

Reference to p. 180
Daily One Minute Meditation

DAY 66

WITNESS YOUR FEARS

Fear is one of our most challenging emotions. It can be overwhelming and complex. You may want to hide from yourself because of the fear you feel. You can be afraid of heights, dogs, certain foods, or people, just to name a few. Fear comes in all kinds of forms. You could have nightmares, scary thoughts, anxiety, and panic attacks. Fear leads to other emotions too. Sometimes, you might think you are angry or sad about a situation, but you may be dealing with hidden fear. Let's say you feel angry toward a colleague for saying something nasty to you in front of another colleague, and your anger is obvious. You may fear this colleague will share this episode with others. You may feel judgmental. A voice may start shouting in times of fear and you feel fright, anger, or shame. This happens to all of us. Something, at some point, will trigger your fears.

So, how do you deal with your fear? Witness the fear. Identify it and reflect on the following questions: "Where is this fear coming from? What are the odds this fear will come true?"

Margaret, a physics teacher, was afraid she would get heart disease, just like her father. *"My father had heart disease and this brought on great fear. I loved him so much that I was worried and stressed for him all the time. I imagined that I would also get heart disease. I always liked to run and hike, but I was afraid that it might affect my heart, so I chose not to do it. My father turned 70, and he was still doing well. It was then that I realized I would not let my fears overwhelm me any longer. I was in my late thirties, and I decided to follow my dreams and, slowly, I started to run and hike. I am now feeling better than ever. Witnessing my fear was the lesson I learned. I decided to look at the future through the lens of hope and leave the fears behind."*

Margaret engaged her class in a debate on how to overcome fears in. At the end of the debate, students drew the most important conclusions about fear:

When you witness your fear, you can deal with it.

2. Define your fear clearly; don't let your fear define you.

3. Make a plan of actions to overcome your fears.

Your mind is often cluttered with thoughts about fear, judgment, anger, and endless possibilities of other emotions. Fear is the projection of your worries into the future. Love, kindness, and compassion will help you overcome your fears.

DAILY PRACTICE

Think of a fear that haunts you most often. Maybe you are afraid of heights, afraid to be rejected or abandoned.

How does it affect you?

How will it affect you next week? Next year? In five years?

Now look at the present moment and imagine you live without this fear.

How do you feel? Take this feeling with you and plan one simple action to reduce the fear.

Reference to p. 180
Daily One Minute Meditation

DAY 67

BE CONFIDENT IN YOURSELF

When you trust and believe in yourself, you connect with the love within you, recognize your strengths and weaknesses and focus on your strengths. You understand how your thoughts influence the way you relate to yourself, why you choose to do things the way you do, and how your decisions impact your life.

Did you ever think about why it is hard for you to decide, to risk, to be curious or spontaneous? If you lack the power to do so, you can become stressed and overwhelmed. Sometimes, you may feel confused, lost, and stuck; you don't trust yourself. How can you overcome this? Practicing mindfulness and relaxation techniques develops a mindset of self-confidence.

In order to build your trust, respect who you are. Respecting yourself is the foundation for you to grow. Respect includes love and kindness, forgiveness, compassion, and appreciation. We all deserve these qualities, but, as with everything else, the process begins within. Accept who you are and cherish your unique qualities. You will feel happier and you will radiate this happiness toward those who surround you. Your students will follow your example and treat you in the same manner. Read Gabriela's story below to see how she learned to trust her emotions. Be aware of how your body responds to your emotions.

Gabriela, a middle-school geography teacher and a mother of two young boys, has taught for ten years and has had many successful students throughout her teaching career. She had every reason to be self-confident, yet it was hard for her to face difficult situations. One day, when she was sitting at her desk, thinking about all the tasks she had to complete and all the issues she had to address, she suddenly felt overwhelmed; stress was pushing down on her shoulders like a heavy burden. Her body had shrunk in a position that made her back ache. She realized she had been sitting in the same position for quite some time only when a student came to her and asked, *"Are you OK, Miss* Gabriela?"

Gabriela realized her negative thoughts and emotions influenced her entire body. She was hunched over and her back was bent. Instead of complicating the situation, she chose to straighten her back. This was a simple solution. She lifted her head, straightened her back, and acknowledged her feelings. She decided to overcome her negative thoughts, to pay attention to her body, by listening to its signs and connecting it with her emotions. From that moment on, when she was overwhelmed by negative thoughts, she stood up straight and focused on her breath. It was a small step towards trust and self-confidence, and she would take it every time she needed.

She shared her practice with her students, so that each time they faced a challenge, they could be confident in themselves, not allowing their body to bend.

DAILY PRACTICE

Become aware of your body and its connection to your emotions. Reflect on how your body reacts to your emotions. Whenever you feel doubtful, focus on your position, stand up straight, and face your emotions. Look ahead for solutions with confidence and trust.

Reference to p. 180
Daily One Minute Meditation

DAY 68

BUILD EMOTIONAL RESILIENCE

Emotional resilience can overcome daily stress and address the challenges in your life. You can always develop your emotional resilience further, in order to achieve a happy and harmonious life. As we stated in Chapter 5, resilience means to bounce forward in difficult moments, to accept and learn from your mistakes, and to move on with courage and trust.

We are all different; we all react differently to the same challenge. Yet, we can all develop resilience. We addressed resilience in Level Three – *Actions*. Let's add three additional actions to build resilience: perseverance, optimism, and positive attitude.

It takes perseverance to achieve your goal. It is not enough to be aware of the importance of perseverance and to create strategies. You have to maintain your driving force and be persistent until your goal is achieved. You need the mindset of the winner: never give up; if you persevere, you will eventually reach your goal, even if you have to put extra effort in it.

Optimism reinforces perseverance. It will always help you bounce forward and find the power within to reach your goal. You can be an optimist or a pessimist. It depends on your conscious mindset to overcome negativity and choose optimism. Think about how this will improve your life.

Your positive attitude builds emotional resilience alongside with perseverance and optimism. Positive attitude helps you find solutions and look at the same challenge from a different perspective when everything else fails. You can boost your positive attitude with a smile that can give you the energy to keep going on when you are ready to give up. A simple smile has many benefits. Your mind cannot make the difference between a real and a fake smile; the benefits are the same. A smile helps you build emotional resilience.

Experts' studies show that healthy children laugh 400 times a day, compared with average adults who laugh less than 15 times a day. These figures are alarming!

Let's practice smiles and laughter, and bring humor back into our lives! This is the best fuel for our mind and body! Release anger, negative emotions, and get back on track to building your emotional resilience with a SMILE.

DAILY PRACTICE

What can be the best supporter of your perseverance, optimism, and positive attitude? It's the smile on your face.

Create the following classroom routine: "Smile when you enter the classroom."

Reference to p. 180
Daily One Minute Meditation

DAY 69

BE AWARE OF YOUR CONCERNS

You will get negative thoughts that could impair your emotional well-being. Your inner conflicts and the conflicts with others can escalate into acts of anger and frustration which can create a negative reaction hurting you and others. How can you acknowledge your emotions and make them your friends, instead of your enemies? Consider how your emotions can serve you.

In Chapter 4, we addressed our emotions through the lens of The Five Core Concerns: status, affiliation, autonomy, role, and appreciation.

Beth, a teacher of art and design, created a visual model to deal with conflict situations. Using the palm of her hand, she created a visual approach to the *Five Core Concerns*, called *Give Me Five*. She named each finger so she could visualize them. *"My thumb became my* Autonomy *because it was separated from the rest of the fingers and represented the decision maker. Then, I named my pointer* Role *because as I point my finger, I am making choices. I need to choose my roles carefully. My middle finger is my* Status *because it stands tall. We all want our status to rise, I thought. My ring finger became my* Affiliation *because it is often the symbol of unity, such as a wedding ring. My pinky is small and sometimes unnoticed, but so very important to my hand. Pinkie, the little finger, became my* Appreciation. *Even if it is the smallest, its contribution is big, bringing balance, charm and completes the palm of my hand."*

"When I have a conflict, I look at my fingers and acknowledge them as my Five Core Concerns. Usually, I look at my pointer first and ask myself, "Is there a problem with my role? What do I need to do to get it back?" Then, I go through each finger. What about my status? Is my autonomy affected? Do I have the right affiliations? Do I lack appreciation? Even though each finger is a different size, they are all connected, working together to accomplish

my needs. I even grade my findings and decide which is the weakest in the chain and then I deal with this challenge using this approach.

This technique adds kinesthetic, visual, and auditory learning to Beth's model that delivers a deeper understanding of her concerns. It also adds depth to understand her emotions and stimulate the positive ones. If you can do this, you will know how to deal with a large number of positive and negative emotions and avoid being overwhelmed.

Hand with concerns – Take Hold of Your Concerns

DAILY PRACTICE

Think of a recent conflict. Spend one minute reflecting on your emotions. Don't judge them, just write them down. Now think again of the conflict. Examine it through Beth's model. Identify which of your concerns affected you most. Identify the other four and the reason you chose the first one as the most important. Address the concern, not the related emotion. Take action to fix the situation.

Reference to p. 180
Daily One Minute Meditation

DAY 70

TEACH FROM YOUR HEART

Take a moment for self-reflection to find the qualities you need inside you so that you can teach from your heart. When you get to know yourself and bring love, kindness, and compassion into your life, your mind fills with positive thoughts and emotions. Negative emotions are also there anyway, but, if you learn how to manage them, you will be able to be confident and bounce forward when a situation gets out of hand.

As teachers, we will put ourselves last, behind the daily needs of our students. However, when you reach emotional balance, you will look at your priorities and find there is more in you than you can ever imagine. You focus on yourself, and you connect with your intuition. Emotional balance gives you an improved sense of being present in the moment; you become more active, and you make better decisions. When you are aware of your emotions, you will find the real sense of right and wrong. You will master empathy, the ability to focus on others, and will see the big picture that includes you too.

The Five Core Concerns model helps you gain your balance and deal with the concern, not with the emotions, especially when you deal with negative concerns that make you become reactive and consume your energy. The Five Core Concerns model also helps you stimulate positive emotions, improve your relationships, and become a better manager of your life.

When you accept and enjoy who you are, you become the architect of the conscious classroom where you have a deep impact on your students and teach from your heart!

DAILY PRACTICE

Think about your classroom and picture yourself in it. Imagine you are the mirror of your classroom. Everything you do and say, the way you are, is reflected in your students' eyes. Think about what you like and what you want to improve in the picture you see.

Make a list of the things that make you feel great and accomplish one every day!

Reference to p. 180
Daily One Minute Meditation

CHAPTER EIGHT

YOUR PHYSICAL WELL-BEING

In Chapter 8, we posit that health, happiness, and fulfillment are key factors contributing to our physical well-being. We will help you adjust your self-perception and guide you towards a new way to live a healthy life.

When your mind is filled with positive thoughts, you project these thoughts toward your body and they become your reality. Your healthy living habits impact you as a teacher. Your nutrition, physical activity, and sleep patterns influence your well-being and, therefore, impact your teaching. When you feel good, you are full of energy and enjoy work. When you do not feel good, your bad disposition will have a negative impact on your students.

Over the next ten days, plan to improve your life and notice the mind/body connection.

Day 71. Be Aware of Your Health

Day 72. Choose a Healthy Perception of Well-Being

Day 73. Show Will Power and Commitment

Day 74. Commit to Change

DAY 71

BE AWARE OF YOUR HEALTH

Focus your attention on your body today. Reflect on your health; are you satisfied with your physical health? Pay attention to your thoughts. Awareness begins with you, with the person you see every day in the mirror when you wash your face, brush your teeth, and get ready for work. But how often do you go beyond these routines and examine your image in the mirror? This is the image you project all day; it is the image your family, your colleagues, and your students will see. Any sign of joy, happiness, discomfort or suffering is reflected on your face, mostly in your eyes. Everybody will notice this. Be aware of your facial expressions and keep the spark in your eyes alive. The way you live your life is a direct reflection of the way you see yourself.

What actions would you take to improve your health? How will these actions affect you on the long run? This is a day to reflect on your lifestyle and on the effects of your habits on your health.

Let's begin with body awareness and recall the quote, "If the body is not cultivated, the mind cannot be cultivated." We all need to eat, to sleep, and to be active rather than sedentary. Most of the time we take our body for granted, and we don't pay attention to its signs, except when there's discomfort, pain, or sickness. We often concentrate on the body part that hurts; however, we need to be aware of our whole body in order to keep it healthy. If we pay attention to our body, we can learn from its signals and reach for well-being.

DAILY PRACTICE

Facial massage can help you relax your body, feel good, and it also has a beneficial psychological effect.

Take three minutes to give yourself a face massage. Give your face comfort and care. Treat it gently. Start with your temples and gently message them. Then move to your cheeks. Rub your hands until they heat up and place them over your eyes for a few seconds, while repeating a positive affirmation such as: "all is well," "I feel the positive energy in my body."

ONE MINUTE MEDITATION FOR CHAPTER 8

Find a comfortable seated position.

Close your eyes or lower your gaze.

Rest your hands in your lap, palms up.

Bring your awareness to your breath.

Inhale through your nose for 4 counts.

Exhale through your mouth for 6 counts.

Think about your face down to the smallest details.

Think about your body down to the smallest details.

Send good thoughts to yourself.

May I be happy.

May I be healthy.

May I be loved.

Look for the spark of health and happiness in your eyes.

Hold on to this image for 30 seconds while you breathe normally.

Bring your awareness back to your breath.

Inhale through your nose for 4 counts.

Exhale through your mouth for 6 counts.

Smile while you slowly open your eyes!

DAY 72

CHOOSE A HEALTHY PERCEPTION OF WELL-BEING

Mindfulness and resilience practices can help you generate positive thoughts about your health. From a simple headache to major health problems, the way you handle the pain and discomfort makes a difference. Your thoughts and emotions lead to a positive or negative perception of the discomfort, but you can always choose the lens you look through. You may choose the lens of pain and suffering, thus allowing the condition to take over your life or you may choose the lens of well-being, perceiving the condition less aggravating, thus not allowing it to take over your life.

How do you describe the way you feel when you are sick? How aware are you of your thoughts and emotions connected to your pain? Deirdre and Fred are both math teachers in the same school. Deirdre has a sore throat, while Fred goes to the hospital to get treatment for his stomach ulcer.

Deirdre has a negative way of perceiving her health problems which makes her become frustrated and short-tempered. Her mood has an impact on her students; they all get the brunt of her sickness.

Fred maintains a good atmosphere in the classroom, regardless of his discomfort, and doesn't let his students be affected by his health problems.

Deidre, whose perception is negative, focuses on her problems and her pain takes over her entire being. Furthermore, it affects her teaching and her students. On the other hand, Fred, whose perception is positive, doesn't let his pain rule his life. He can stay objective, focus on his most important tasks, and control the level of his discomfort.

The way you look at challenges and pain makes all the difference; it depends on your perception of health and well-being.

Happy Teacher's Glasses

When your thoughts are positive, you don't feed the pain but rather accept it and find solutions to address it. Negative thoughts will increase your pain. If you change the way you think about pain, both your body and your mind respond differently. It's your decision to choose positive thoughts over the negative ones and to see your life through the lens of well-being.

DAILY PRACTICE

Mindfulness practices can help you heal. Conscious breathing practices may help you change your focus and release the pain.

Inhale deeply, hold your breath for a few seconds and exhale. You can use words or phrases to guide you. For example, when you inhale, you can say: "I bring peace in" and when you exhale: "I release tension."

Practice conscious breathing for 4-6 times. This may help you choose the lens of well-being when you look at your health.

Reference to p. 205
Daily One Minute Meditation

DAY 73

SHOW WILL POWER AND COMMITMENT

The process of transformation in your life goes through different phases. When you become aware of your health issues and you decide to make a change for the better, your willpower and commitment help you carry it out. Different people respond to change in different ways. Look at the process of change from the following two perspectives: you can do it alone, being your own partner, or you need other people's partnership. As you read them, think about what option fits you best.

1. You recognize the need and you have the strength to take action by yourself. This assumes you have the inner motivation even during tough times. You are mindful and resilient, and, if you make a mistake, you will still continue. You want to embrace the experience alone. You are driven internally.

2. You recognize the need to act, but you know yourself and you aren't the type of person who can take action without a partner's guidance and support. So, you look for the right person who encourages you to succeed, a person who is kind, mindful of your concerns, and sensitive to your personal situation. This person needs to be honest with you and compassionate. You work better with a partner; yet, you are still determined to change.

Both situations help you know yourself better. It's not a sign of a big ego if you can do it by yourself, nor is it a sign of weakness if you need a partner.

It's hard for any of us to change. It takes courage to admit who we are and do it the right way. Read Joel's story and think about how it can inspire you.

Joel, a high school teacher, wanted to share his story with us: *"Throughout my childhood, my parents were always busy with their jobs, trying to provide for us the best way they could. Having food on the table was one of their main worries, and they didn't care much about anything else. They didn't have time for me and my problems. They both were overweight and so was I. I was bullied by my peers, had low grades in school, and chose friends with no self-esteem. So, I believed I was doomed. I was impulsive and nothing worked. Even if I thought about change from time to time, I couldn't find the way and the motivation to make a change. Then I had a breakthrough. I was 17 and a teacher asked me what grudges I was carrying. I had no idea what she was talking about, but she wouldn't give up on me. She guided me to break out with the past - I was a worthwhile human being. This teacher, Mrs. Butler, changed my life, but she couldn't have done it without me! She asked me what was important to me. She saw in me the spark I never knew I had. She wouldn't accept the words I kept repeating: "I've tried so many times and it never works for me. Others can change, but not me! You have no idea how many times I have tried to change." She wouldn't give up on me and she taught me to trust myself. That's why I am a high-school teacher today, just like Mrs. Butler. I made a commitment back then to help others the way she helped me. Don't let your life, the only one you have, go to waste. Don't wait until you get sick to fix yourself. You may not have a Mrs. Butler, but you have yourself. Your students need you to model positive behavior just as Mrs. Butler did for me. She made a difference!"* Joel couldn't make the change by himself. However, when he accepted guidance, support, and encouragement, he managed to change his life for the better.

If you become aware of your needs, you may become aware of your strengths and weaknesses. You learn to accept them without judgment, so you can commit to achieve your goal. You let go of the guilt and shame and accept guidance and support on your path of transformation. Furthermore, if you have the courage to share your experience, you will role model willpower and commitment.

DAILY PRACTICE

Think about how you deal with change. Do you recognize yourself in scenario one or two? Accept who you are and don't judge others who are not like you.

Share this story with your students and emphasize that each of us is different.

Reference to p. 205
Daily One Minute Meditation

DAY 74

COMMIT TO CHANGE

Think about the most important things in your life. Even if you don't realize at the beginning, you will eventually find that your health needs to be at the top of the list. Your healthy habits impact you daily and affect your teaching. When you are healthy, everything works well. You can work with ease and your stress level is low. However, there may be times when you are not well; your energy level is low and you think your days are longer than usual. These are the times you may realize you need to make a change to live a fulfilling and healthy life.

The way you think is the key to change; the way you perceive the situation will determine the results. Your negative thoughts stream into your consciousness... *I can't do this, I don't have time to do that, I wish my life were different*. Once you become aware of these negative thoughts, you can take charge of your life. Ask yourself whether it is important for you to make the change. Think about it. You may immediately see all the reasons you can't change. Once you become aware of the reasons, you can determine what is stopping you. Define the importance of change.

Are you ready to take the step forward and turn your thoughts into actions? For some people, it is easy and natural to take action. They are the lucky ones who decide something and go for it. The goal is achieved and they can enjoy the outcome. However, this doesn't work for all of us. Sometimes, we get stuck at decision making stage and delay or postpone the action we need to take. We might even create a new deadline. Have you ever said, *"On Monday, I will reduce my sugar intake? Or increase the amount of exercise I do? Or get the sleep I need?"* You may procrastinate – listen to the voice in your head that says "put things on hold until later!" Procrastination can affect different aspects of our life, including physical health and well-being. It involves self-deception; you experience guilt and unhappiness that lead to anxiety and depression.

You have to fight and beat procrastination in your head first! Mindfulness practices and resilience skills keep your thoughts positive. Breathing exercises and meditation will release the stress and help you focus on your goals. Your thought process is your key to change. Consider the situation is a challenge not a problem.

DAILY PRACTICE

Reflect on procrastination today.

Make a list with the three most important things you want to accomplish in one year. Take one you've been procrastinating for a while and make it your priority. Decide to take one action to beat procrastination and commit to that action. Reward yourself every time you've achieved your goal.

Reference to p. 205
Daily One Minute Meditation

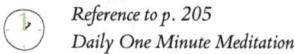

DAY 75

PRACTICE ROUTINES FOR A HEALTHY LIFE

Once you have decided to live a healthy life, you need to develop healthy habits. A habit is a set of regular and repeated behaviors. If you are a walker and you walk five miles a day, then that's a great habit. But if you are a smoker, it's not such a good habit. Habits are supported by routines. Many of us follow the same routines over and over again to support our habits. It is not easy to break old habits, such as smoking, drinking, and overeating. If you want to give up on your old, unwanted habits, you need to start by changing your routines. You have to be consistent and take the transformational actions. In time, this leads to an enhanced state of well-being.

Routines are formed in your mind, and they are connected to your thoughts and emotions. Once you transform them into actions, they become a set of activities that give you confidence and trust and build your self-esteem. Routines can last for a set period of time (e.g., you walk for 30 minutes every day). When you form a new routine, you need to commit to it. In time, it becomes an unconscious action that you automatically include in your life. Always be aware of your routines and empower the positive ones.

Anna is an assistant teacher, studying to become a full-time teacher. Every year, she kept delaying her exams, not having enough time to study and take her degree. After several years, she became exhausted and lost her enthusiasm. *"I realized I had to make a change. I wasn't getting anywhere doing what I was doing. So, I analyzed my habits and my daily routines and made a list to see what I needed to do in order to manage my time better and finish my studies. I focused on my positive habits nurturing a healthy lifestyle. I became aware that I did have good eating habits, but I didn't spend enough time exercising and my sleeping schedule was too short, having less than six hours of sleep daily. I realized this was the reason why I felt tired all the time and couldn't focus on my studies. I created a routine to include specific time for me to exercise, and I also cut my time on social media so I could increase my sleeping schedule to a minimum of 7 hours. It wasn't easy to stick to the routine in the first 21 days, but it was worth the effort. I had a lot more energy, and I also became motivated to study. After all, I wanted so much the degree to become a full time teacher! That was my motivating factor."*

With a clear goal in mind, Anna included new routines in her life and stuck to them along the following guidelines:

- Check your progress at the end of each day.
- Don't give up if you weren't successful on a particular day.
- Keep going and celebrate after 21 days.

Anna shared her findings with her peer teachers and students and encouraged them to become aware of their habits and routines: "*It became easier after 21 days and, after 60 days, I had actually created a new set of routines. You can't imagine how my life has changed. Start with changing your routines and stick to it. Whatever you do, make sure you have a very important target that gives you the motivation to change.*"

DAILY PRACTICE

Think about your daily routines? Make a list of the positive ones versus the negative ones and see which way your balance is turning. Create your new set of routines for a healthy lifestyle.

Reference to p. 205
Daily One Minute Meditation

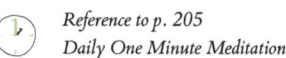

DAY 76

EAT WITH MINDFUL BITES

Your body and health are affected by what you eat. Diabetes, obesity, cancer, heart disease, high blood pressure, and stroke are all major diseases associated in some way to the foods we eat. The eating process is complex – think about how digesting the food becomes easier on your body when you slow down and take notice. It's similar to breathing. Just as you focus on your breath, you may also focus on your eating. The food you eat and your eating patterns were established years ago. You might recall the dinner table when you were growing up. What messages did you get? What thoughts or feelings come to mind? Eating is among the hardest things for us to change; so, be patient with yourself. Take mindful bites and give yourself the joy of eating. Set up your mind to eat mindfully every time.

Let's hear from Jane, a first-grade teacher, who had weight problems all her life and decided to reconsider her eating habits. She slowly changed them by focusing on her thoughts first, then on her actions. She took small actions that led her to a healthy routine.

"I know the food I eat can affect my lifespan. Yet, I wasn't able to figure out how to make a change and start to eat healthy foods. I observed that I was always eating under stress, gobbled down my food and had no control over the quality or quantity of the food. This was the moment when I realized, I needed to change my eating habits. I decided to switch to mindful eating. I focused on the way the food looked, tasted, smelled, and I thought about how it was going to help me stay healthy. I created my own mindfulness eating practice. Here is exactly what I do: I look at the food before I start to eat. My intention is to use all of my senses as I eat. I put my food on a smaller plate. I make sure I chew the food slowly, and I notice how the flavor changes. It still amazes me what a different experience this is. That was three years ago. Now, I eat mindfully at all times. As a result, I have changed my eating habits. I am not sure when it all happened because it was a process and it just flowed."

Beside eating, you may also consider becoming aware of your daily hydration needs. Food and water are the fuels that keep your body functioning all day. Make sure that you drink at least six glasses of water daily. It will make you feel more energetic, and you will do your body a big favor.

You can enhance your state of well-being and improve your health if you create your own routines for mindful eating and hydrating.

DAILY PRACTICE

Jane explored her family history and knew she had several family members with nutrition related diseases. Her advice is: Look at the following nutrition related diseases and check off those in your family:

Diabetes ______

Obesity ______

Cancer ______

Heart Disease ______

High Blood Pressure or Hypertension ______

Stroke ______

Tooth decay ______

Kidney Disease ______

Arteriosclerosis ______

Other ______

Become aware of the factors influencing your health. What is one action you can take today to develop a simple routine that could lead you to a healthier diet?

Reference to p. 205
Daily One Minute Meditation

DAY 77

MOTIVATE YOURSELF TO BECOME PHYSICALLY ACTIVE

Your body is made to be active, not sedentary. Including physical activity in your daily schedule will help your body and your mind thrive, thus providing you with energy throughout the day. Remember the Latin phrase: *Mens sana in corpore sano - a healthy mind in a healthy body.*

Is the level of your physical activity contributing to your good health? Some of us will say 'yes', but, unfortunately, many of us will answer with 'no'. Those who answered *yes* can role-model positive behavior for those who answered *no*. We can always learn from each other!

How can you integrate more activity into your life? Just like all of us, your day is crammed with responsibilities. Your time is limited. Yet, you know you are responsible for your health, and you are the only one who can change your lifestyle.

First, get your mind connected to your body. How often do you stop and feel your body as a whole, from the top of your head all the way down to the tip of your toes? When was the last time you scanned your body, trying to reconnect with it and understand the signs it gives you?

Next, become aware of the environment that best suits you. Think about the following: where do you feel most comfortable, indoors or outdoors? If you were to consider a sport, would it to be an indoor or outdoor sport? Get to know those surroundings that give you the best chance for success.

Now that you have become aware of the connections between your mind, body, and environment, it's time to consider the idea that you can add physical activity to your life. If you already do this, you may share your good practice with others and invite them to join you. If you haven't started it yet, you may consider embracing the following thought: *I can have an active life*. This doesn't mean that you will have to start tomorrow to workout for hours; you can start with simple steps. Just think, "My goal is to develop a healthy habit. This habit will give my body more oxygen and will generate more energy for me." You need to transform this thought into a habit.

Let's consider Marina's example, a fourth grade teacher. She realized she was living a very sedentary life, and she decided to take action and change.

Marina drove her car to school every day and parked on the closest available spot she found in front of the building. She took the elevator whenever she had to go upstairs and sat on her chair most of the time when she was teaching. One day, she arrived late at school and the only parking place she found was behind the building, far away from the entrance. She made her way to the elevator, where she saw the sign: "out of order." She furiously climbed the stairs all the way to her classroom on the third floor and felt exhausted. She could barely catch her breath. She thought, "*This doesn't look like a good start of the day*!"

Fortunately, this "not such a good day" turned out to be the best day to start the change. She realized she couldn't continue cheating herself. Her health was important, and she knew she had to get out of her comfort zone to make a change. She started with a new routine of walking up the stairs instead of using the elevator and added more walking to her daily schedule. Marina shared he experience with her colleagues and created a movement for health improvement in school, called "Each step counts for my health."

Every change starts in your mind. You need the power within to transform your thoughts into words and actions. Walking, swimming, jogging, and bicycling are all activities you may consider to improve your health. Exercises can lower your blood pressure, reduce your stress level, and strengthen your heart and lungs. Make physical activities part of your daily routine!

DAILY PRACTICE

Consider those activities you are attracted to. What kind of activity would you like to do? Is it strength training, aerobic conditioning, yoga? Do you like to walk, run or swim? What feels right for you?

Select a physical activity you like to start doing and make a plan to start doing it. Create a set of routines to support your plan.

Examples: "I will walk 10,000 steps every day." "I will exercise every Tuesday and Thursday from 6 to 7."

As we mentioned before, routines are your support to develop healthy habits.

Reference to p. 205
Daily One Minute Meditation

DAY 78

ENSURE "A GOOD NIGHT'S SLEEP"

Besides healthy eating and exercising habits, healthy sleep habits also contribute to your well-being. A good night's sleep fills you up with energy and your whole day can be different.

Specialists recommend between 7-8 hours of sleep per night. When you lack sleep, your body doesn't function to its best capacity and your mind cannot focus. It's not only you who will suffer; the negative impact will also be reflected on your teaching, affecting your students and colleagues. Therefore, you have to become aware of your sleeping habits and recognize the need to improve or change them if you have to. You will get the reward during the day when you experience more energy and enthusiasm.

Carl, a drama teacher, has had difficulty sleeping for years, slowly losing his enthusiasm and motivation to teach. He was unhappy. He shared with us his thoughts: "*I was always tired. I never got a good night's sleep. I kept tossing and turning all night. I knew I had to do something. I started to analyze my thoughts, behaviors and the environment which held me back from having a good night's sleep.*"

Carl decided he was going to change his sleep habits. He used a mindful approach to it. "*Once I decided to be mindful of my sleeping habits, I acknowledged the times when I had a good night's sleep and those times when I didn't. I looked at my bedroom and the place where I was sleeping. I indulged myself with a comfortable bed and pillows. The hardest decision was to free my bedroom from technology. I set up a lower temperature for sleeping and I changed my window shutters to block the light coming into the room.*

Next, I wrote a to-do list for a relaxing bedtime routine to help me sleep better. I'd like to share it with you – maybe you can use some of my tips yourself:

Carl's routines for a good night's sleep:

1. Focus on your breath or use one of the breathing techniques to allow your body to relax. Use meditation for a restful sleep, called 4/7/8

2. Let go of your thoughts of fear and worry as you lie in bed as if they were clouds floating by. Just watch them float.

3. Bring thoughts of gratitude and choose three things you are grateful for at the end of everyday. Focus on your gratitude.

4. Do a progressive body relaxation to release pressure and tension from your body, such as Yoga Nidra meditation.

With his new approach to sleeping, Carl became aware of the times when he had a good night's sleep and of those when he was facing difficulties. He switched his mindset toward a positive thinking pattern, giving himself the message that he will be able to sleep instead of worrying that he won't. Most people who can't sleep well send themselves repetitive negative messages before going to bed, such as: *"I can't sleep," "I will wake up in the middle of the night," "I know that I will not be able to sleep well,"* etc. Once you become aware of your thinking patterns, you may change them into positive affirmations to help your mind set up for a good night's sleep.

DAILY PRACTICE

Be aware of your sleeping habits.

If you are a good sleeper, acknowledge it and be grateful for it.

If you are not, try to find the solution that works best for you, before going on medication. You may try a classic breathing exercise every time that will help you calm and relax your body in both situations. Dr. Andrew Weil, internationally-recognized expert for his views on leading a healthy life, called this exercise a "natural tranquilizer for the nervous system."

MEDITATION FOR A RESTFUL SLEEP
CALLED… 4/7/8

Close your eyes.

Inhale through your nose while you count to 4.

Pause while you count to 7.

Exhale while you count to 8.

Repeat this exercise 6 times.

Reference to p. 205
Daily One Minute Meditation

DAY 79

MENTAL FITNESS

After having discussed routines for a healthy physical lifestyle, we will look into the necessity of topping it with a healthy mindset. Mental exercises stimulate the brain just as physical exercises stimulate the body. When you challenge your mind by doing new things, you become more alert and mentally fit, using both the right and left side of our brain. The left side is the analytical, rational, and goal oriented one. You may see the work you put in your lesson plans, checklists, and everything you do to become better organized, in a different perspective, if you realize these are exercises that strengthen the left side of your brain.

The right side is the intuitive, emotional, creative, and artistic part of the brain. To strengthen the right side of the brain, you can talk about your emotions with your friends and family members. You can also say to your students: *I am happy today! How are you feeling?* Positive emotions have an impact on your face and body, they release the tension and you will radiate joy and happiness. Show positive emotions to others. They are contagious and people will show positive emotions when you interact with them.

Physical exercises can improve your brain performance. There are certain exercises that are more helpful to the brain than others. Jogging and swimming improve cardiovascular fitness and help your entire body, including your brain, to function more efficiently. However, if you want to actually enhance your brain functions, you should concentrate on balance and exercises that strengthen your legs, such as tennis, basketball, or dance.

Mental fitness is your choice and it is an important part of your good health. Don't get into the habit of doing always the same thing, in the same way, over and over again. Challenge yourself. Think about both sides of your brain when you make small changes in your lifestyle. Body and mind should always be in balance to bring you the enthusiasm and energy to stay positive in your teaching.

Your social connections can enhance your mental fitness. It requires actively thinking about yourself and about the other person. You can ask someone to partner with you to do daily exercises together. Surround yourself with people who resonate with you and value who you are. This makes your life more fulfilling and happier.

DAILY PRACTICE

Remove obstacles! Take risks and do new things to become mentally fit. See obstacles as challenges for a new project.

Choose one project that interests you. Make a list of obstacles that may stand in the way of completing your project. Choose one obstacle and make it a challenge to accomplish your project.

Reference to p. 205
Daily One Minute Meditation

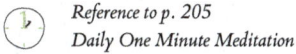

DAY 80

TAKE PRIDE IN YOUR GOLDEN LINES

Your overall well-being consists of your mental, emotional, and physical well-being. When you listen to your body and mind, you will get the right signals and build the awareness of your needs.

Reflect on your personal story and don't let anything hold you back from your personal transformation. Be open to the change within. Your story will be different from other people's stories. Each of us chooses his/her own way. The right process for you lies within you. A mindset of well-being is a big step toward your transformation. It can open the door to change.

You can learn from your failures and mistakes. No one is spared such episodes. With our failures, there are moments when we feel unworthy and not valued by others. During those times, you may feel your life is falling apart and you are out of control. This can take us back to the story of the Japanese broken pots, Kintsukuroi (to repair with gold).

Five hundred years ago, in Japan, there was a technique to restore broken pots. The artists glued together all the broken pieces. They highlighted the repair lines with golden dye. They made this golden dye vivid and they didn't hide any parts of the broken lines. These golden lines gave the broken pots a new design, restoring the pot to something more beautiful, emphasizing the magnificence of the regained wholeness. Imagine how extraordinary these broken pots became. They symbolized something more beautiful than the original.

When you paraphrase this story, you can recognize the pot in your life tells your story which is filled with adventure and magnificence. Don't be afraid to show your weaknesses and vulnerabilities. If you learn and accept them, they become part of who you are.

Those golden lines outline you and become your pride showing you can stand back up, make the change you need, and put your life back together.

Take an action that works for you – it can open your door to change. Like a Japanese pot, your balance comes from within. Everything you think, feel, eat, and do for your health matters and keeps you together as a whole. Your lessons for change will be marked with gold.

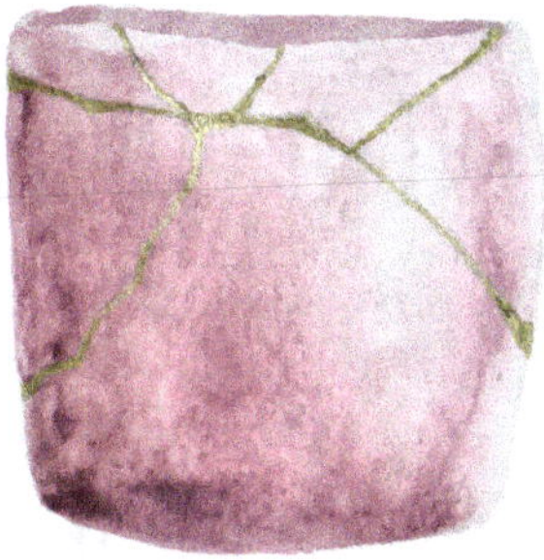

Japanese broken pots, Kintsukuroi – Open Yourself to Change

DAILY PRACTICE

Think about yourself. Imagine your life as the Japanese pot. What are the fracture lines you were trying to hide, trying to look perfect on the outside? Envision them and highlight them with gold, so you can use them as your guidelines and learn from them. Share this exercise with your students.

Reference to p. 205
Daily One Minute Meditation

CHAPTER NINE

YOUR AUTHENTIC VOICE

The previous chapters have taken you on a journey of self-discovery and introspection. In this chapter, you continue your journey as you discover your authentic voice. Your voice is unique and represents your honest thoughts, emotions, and feelings. You choose what you say.

Sometimes, however, you may find yourself speaking words that don't represent you. Perhaps those words come from a place of fear, anger, or even shame. We all experience this, at times. When you are aware of yourself, you recognize your strengths and weaknesses and value your own truth; your words follow through, reflect who you are, and your voice becomes authentic.

The authentic voice is linked to your identity and is empowered by your vision. If you are true to yourself, you speak honestly and you take full responsibility for the words you use to send your message.

Every word you speak sends impulses to your students' minds. If you know how to make your words matter, your students will listen to you and they will recognize your authenticity.

For the next ten days of this chapter, you will explore ways to empower your voice.

Day 81. Express Authenticity

Day 82. Speak with Integrity

Day 83. Develop the "Time Factor" for Authentic Communication

Day 84. Speak and Listen with Compassion

Day 85. Take Care of Your Voice

Day 86. Know Your Spoken and Written Voice

Day 87. Practice the *Traffic Light* for Good Communication

Day 88. Follow the *Golden Rule* for Authentic Communication

Day 89. Verbal and Non-verbal Communication

Day 90. The Authentic Voice of the Teacher Within

DAY 81

EXPRESS AUTHENTICITY

Have you ever felt at a loss of words? Have you started to say something at a staff meeting but couldn't express yourself? Or have you ever wanted to tell your students something, but the words you spoke were different from what you had intended? By the time you realized you misspoke, the moment passed and the window of opportunity was lost. All these examples point toward your search for your authentic voice.

Authenticity means that you are genuinely acknowledging your own truth. You are consistent with the message you send. Your words come from your heart and show your vulnerability. You express your authenticity through your ability to encourage your students to think and share their opinions. You listen to them with empathy for their concerns and feelings. All these characteristics lead toward good communication, the ultimate goal of a mindful teacher.

Peg, a middle school science teacher, described her experience in the quest for her authentic voice. "*I came to this school to teach middle school science after five years of experience as a college teacher. I have always followed my vision and set up high expectations for myself and my students. My vision was: make students understand and feel comfortable with the information. A few months later, I realized that my students didn't understand the concepts I had been teaching. I hadn't adapted my teaching style to their age-group. It was not easy, but I had to do something different. Guided by my vision, I developed a deeper understanding of my students' needs. I rephrased my messages so they became clearer and stronger; I asked my students to repeat what I said, so I could be sure they 'got it'. I used a friendly and supportive voice to encourage their learning."* Peg found her authentic voice so she could stay true to her vision and drew the following conclusions:

Your authentic voice is empowered by your vision and is:

- Honest and confident
- Empathic and patient
- Intuitive to identify your students' needs

As a mindful and resilient teacher, you undergo a transformative change that gives your voice authenticity. You speak honestly and continue to uphold your beliefs. With this in mind, let's reflect on the characteristics of an authentic voice.

DAILY PRACTICE

Breathing exercises can help relax your body and your vocal cords, giving your message a pleasant and confident tone.

Try the following breathing exercise to soothe and empower your tone of voice:

Stand straight with your legs hip-width apart and your feet pointing forward. Inhale while slowly counting to two. Exhale for twice as long as you inhaled, while counting to four. Gaze ahead for ten seconds and raise your arms while you continue breathing. Relax your shoulders and let your arms slowly float down to your sides. Say your name aloud. Say it again. Hear the sound of your voice. Hear the intonation. No one else sounds exactly like you. Say your name again. Give gratitude to your voice.

Make a statement to empower your voice; e.g., "My voice is soft and calm." "My voice is warm and friendly."

Say your name again with your statement in your mind. Feel the difference.

Daily One Minute Meditation

ONE MINUTE MEDITATION FOR CHAPTER 9

Find a comfortable seated position.

Close your eyes or lower your gaze.

Rest your hands in your lap, palms facing up.

Bring your awareness to your breath.

Inhale through your nose as you count to 4.

Exhale through your mouth as you count to 6.

Think of the last meaningful discussion you had with someone.

What was the tone of the conversation?

Recall the tone of your voice during the conversation.

Recall the feelings you had towards the other person.

If it was a peaceful conversation, keep the peace within and enjoy the feeling.

If it was a tense conversation, try to eliminate the negative thoughts and bring back your peace of mind.

Acknowledge the way you say things will have a deeper impact than what you say.

Send positive thoughts to the other person.

Bring your attention back to your breath.

Inhale through your nose as you count to 4.

Exhale through your mouth as you count to 6.

Smile as you slowly open your eyes!

DAY 82

SPEAK WITH INTEGRITY

Your life lived with integrity is reflected in your authentic voice and your responsible actions. Your words are authentic and, even if you reject something, your decision will be respected, it will not be taken as a personal offense.

Often, you find yourself in a situation when your first impulse is to say *yes* to different requests, without thinking of how this might affect your time and your own personal commitments; you make promises, saying *yes* to requests you cannot fulfill, and you find yourself procrastinating your own tasks. Fear of affecting a relation and being considered indifferent may drive you to say *yes* rather than assume the responsibility of saying *no*. You speak with integrity when you take responsibility of your words and you know when to say *yes* or *no*. You speak your truth and follow your vision.

Have the courage to say *no* to demands you cannot accept, in order to say *yes* to yourself. Always think of what brings value to your life, what is important to you and how can you live with integrity. Don't try to become a people pleaser and be committed to your goals. It is not selfish to say *no* if you know what is right for you.

Sally's story.

Sally is a fourth-grade teacher, helpful, supportive, never denying a favor to anyone. Sally said, "*I came from a family with high parental expectations, where I was taught to accept all challenges and never upset my parents. My mother raised me to believe if I didn't obey her and do what she asked, I would lose her love and respect. Deep down in my soul, I learned to be nice, a pleaser for everyone around me.*"

One day, when she was with her students at the playground, Sally agreed to watch over some students from a colleague's class.

The number of students was too high for just one teacher and the inevitable happened. "*A student fell off the slide and broke her leg. I was devastated. In that instant, I understood I couldn't live up to other people's expectations. Of course, I didn't want to hurt anyone, so I accepted my colleague's request. However, in doing so, I ended up failing my own duties and, eventually, blaming myself. I realized I couldn't handle things this way anymore. I must be true to myself and have the courage and integrity to do what feels right for me and my students and what I can take full responsibility for.*"

As a teacher, it is important to find strategies to be supportive of your students, to teach them how to recognize their limitations, and to be responsible for their decisions. When you are aligned to your values, saying *no* is the option you may choose over saying *yes* and feeling bad because you are neglecting your responsibilities.

DAILY PRACTICE

There are many decisions you have to make during a school day. Under stress, you sometimes don't have enough time to think them through and assume responsibility for what you have said. Therefore, practicing mindful breathing and meditation can help you lower the stress and make you aware of your thoughts, words, and actions.

MEDITATION

Focus on your breath, let the muscles in your body relax.

Relax your feet, your legs, your stomach, your back, your shoulders, and neck.

Become aware of every part of your body.

Consciously, allow every body part to become relaxed.

Give yourself time to just be.

Become aware of the power within you.

Reconnect with yourself.

Reference to p. 233
Daily One Minute Meditation

DAY 83

DEVELOP THE TIME FACTOR FOR AUTHENTIC COMMUNICATION

Authentic communication comes from within; it is what motivates you and is based on a deeper awareness of your vulnerabilities. Fear can freeze your words and leave you with a bitter taste. Therefore, speak only when you are ready. However, when you have to be spontaneous, make sure you choose your words consciously. If you are like most of us, you experience many moods throughout the day; your moods fluctuate and this may influence your conversations. Be aware of your mood and make sure that when you say something it matters.

When you choose your words carefully and speak at the right time, the words can have the impact you wished for your students. We often say "what you do today will affect you tomorrow." Be aware of the appropriate time to speak and share your ideas.

Authentic communication becomes the foundation of strong and trusting relations. When your voice has a clear message, your students are more likely to understand you. Speak your truth at the right time and have the courage to say what you really believe.

You move toward safety when you focus on the timeliness of what you say. We all know there were times when we said something on the spur of the moment rather than wait! If you have a disagreement with a colleague or a student and you say something at the wrong time, the situation can escalate.

Make your authentic voice aware of the *Time factor*. Ask yourself, "Is this the right time to speak or do I need to be quiet and listen?" Consider a simple technique of counting to ten before your answer. You talk with an authentic voice when you learn to listen first.

Observe the *Time Factor* in communication; speak at the right time for meaningful conversations. Follow these suggestions to guide you:

1. Become aware of your thoughts and emotions. Speak only when your thoughts are not clouded by anger.
2. Take full responsibility of your words and actions. Be true to yourself.
3. Practice self-control and mindful listening to find the right time to speak.
4. Have the courage to speak your truth. You may even choose not to speak at that certain time.
5. When you speak, do it with care and kindness and avoid judgment, blame, gossip, and criticism.

DAILY PRACTICE

Review the 5 suggestions above and reflect on a recent situation when you spoke at the right time. Then, think of a situation in which you spoke and weren't ready. What was the difference? What could you have said differently in the second situation if you had counted to ten before answering?

Reference to p. 233
Daily One Minute Meditation

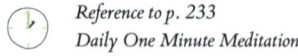

DAY 84

SPEAK AND LISTEN WITH COMPASSION

As you focus on authentic communication and listen to yourself and others, your words show compassion. You seek to understand the other person better and you guide him/her to find the solution by asking the right questions. You are compassionate if you have the desire to help and do not try to fix the other person's problem.

A true test of your authenticity will be when you are faced with negative behavior, and, still, you can understand the other person's situation and show compassion. If you think that you are not able to master the art of compassion yet, you still have learned something new from the experience.

As Tom, a university professor stated, "*I was a professor with all the success and status in the world, but not within myself. I remember when Jean Claude, one of my students, walked into my office, asking for help on an assignment. I got upset and told him to go back to his dorm and get it done. 'You have no reason to come here and ask for help when you could have done this by yourself,' I arrogantly said with a harsh voice. He quietly answered, "Sir, I am sorry, I got distracted. I've just found out that my mother is very sick and has only a few more months to live. She lives quite far from here, in Gabon, Africa. I just want to get my grades up so my Mom could be proud. I really don't understand the assignment." He stood and slightly bowed to me as I looked into his eyes. He was about to walk out of the office when I finally had the strength to say, with a soft voice: I am sorry to hear that. Let's go over the material. Today, you have become my teacher!"*

They have worked together since then. Jean Claude graduated, and Tom has never been the same. Compassion is the uplifting reminder that we all have lessons to learn.

DAILY PRACTICE

Show compassion in your relations. Think of a situation when you acted like Tom. Most of us can relate to his situation. Jean Claude became the venue for Tom to learn about compassion. It is said "the teacher appears when you are ready." In Tom's case, Jean Claude became the teacher for his professor.

What does compassion mean to you?

Reference to p. 233
Daily One Minute Meditation

DAY 85

TAKE CARE OF YOUR VOICE

Teaching may be the profession with the highest occupational voice demands. Your voice is your most important resource. You may not always realize the importance of your voice and, therefore, you may pay less attention to it and abuse it. Just like actors and singers, you too need to protect your voice.

When we speak about the authentic voice of a teacher, we mostly think about the words and the language a teacher uses. However, the authentic voice is not only about the spoken words but also about the vibration of the vocal cords, the tool a teacher uses daily. According to various studies conducted in this field, students don't learn as efficiently from teachers with a raspy voice as they do from teachers who have a healthy and smooth tone of voice.

A mindful teacher is aware of the tone of his/her voice and the impact it has on students. Take care of your voice as you take care of your body. Your body gets tired, so does your voice. Drink water and warm drinks to hydrate your vocal cords. Mindfulness practices can help your voice and your body. You may consider the following suggestions to protect your voice:

- Do daily breathing exercises;
- Spend quiet time or rest your voice when it's not necessary to talk;
- Drink plenty of water.

Pay attention to the changes that may occur in your voice and keep it healthy.

DAILY PRACTICE

How well do you know the sound of your voice when it's healthy? How does your voice sound when you express strong feelings and emotions?

Choose a time to record your voice when you are teaching and listen to it with the following guidelines:

- How does my voice sound?
- What feelings and emotions can I hear in my voice?
- For how long do I keep my normal tone without raising my voice?
- For how long do I speak during a class?

Use your answers to reflect and to take care of your voice in the future. Find your own strategies to protect your valuable asset.

Reference to p. 233
Daily One Minute Meditation

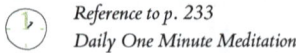

DAY 86

KNOW YOUR SPOKEN AND WRITTEN VOICE

There are several ways to think about your voice. Usually, you think about your vocal cords and the sounds they make so you can be heard. However, you can also think about your voice in terms of your written thoughts, opinions, and ideas.

When you speak, you may not always have the same fluency as when you write. You might make grammar errors or end the sentence improperly while speaking, but, if the idea is well presented, nobody will notice. The spoken language is connected to your body language and your emotions. In written form, your voice is not supported by your emotions; you must express your voice visually to make the same impact. You cannot use the intonation of your voice or body language to enhance the clarity of your message. However, you can edit the words and make the message stronger.

Once you have found your voice, either in speech or in writing, it resonates with the listener or the reader; in their mind, they may think "this is exactly what I was expecting to hear!"

Inspire your students to find their own voice. This can be challenging for them. It will be your responsibility to role model an authentic voice for them to follow. In time, they will find their own voice, whether it is in spoken form or in writing.

DAILY PRACTICE

Reflect on your voice. Which is stronger, your spoken or your written voice? Do you communicate more authentically through speech or through writing? Whichever you choose, your voice is authentic when you speak your truth.

Reference to p. 233
Daily One Minute Meditation

DAY 87

PRACTICE THE TRAFFIC LIGHT FOR GOOD COMMUNICATION

As a teacher, it is your responsibility to create an environment for authentic communication in your classroom. Set up clear rules of communication so your teaching is enjoyable. As a mindful and resilient teacher, you create a warm, friendly, and safe environment.

There are times when, during a conversation, someone interrupts the flow of the conversation. There are also times when you interrupt someone because you feel the urge to communicate your idea right away. Both situations affect your message. You or the other person can end up feeling frustrated. These situations can occur in the classroom as well.

Christina is an elementary school teacher. When we met, some time ago, she mentioned that she had faced difficulties when she allowed her students to have conversations amongst themselves. Although she wanted everybody's voice to be heard, she could not achieve this goal because some students would interrupt others. She set up clear rules for authentic communication. She compared this situation with the traffic light rules:

Red: Stop

Yellow: Listen

Green: Talk

Christina explained the rules to her students:

Stop. In a conversation, it's important to be aware of your place and responsibility in communication. Stop and breathe before you start speaking.

Listen. When you speak to someone, make eye-contact, listen and understand what he or she has to say. Count to ten and take time to think about your words.

Talk. Fully engage in the conversation and use your words carefully so they have a clear message.

Christina's students engaged in this *traffic light* conversation game, and they became aware of their turn in the conversation. The conversations were more meaningful and fun.

DAILY PRACTICE

Reflect on conversations that may take place in your classroom. Use the traffic light rule or create your own set of rules to facilitate authentic communication. Make your students stick to the rules and help your students use them in their everyday life.

Reference to p. 233
Daily One Minute Meditation

DAY 88

FOLLOW THE GOLDEN RULE FOR AUTHENTIC COMMUNICATION

You live in a world based on social interactions; you are not by yourself. Everything you say and do will reflect back at you. The Confucian Golden Rule of Reciprocity reads: "Do not impose on others what you do not wish for yourself." We can paraphrase this maxim to: "Listen and speak to others as you want them to listen and speak to you."

The Golden Rule emphasizes values of mutuality, interdependence, and reciprocity. If you ponder on this idea from the perspective of universal understanding, you realize the Golden Rule can be the foundation for authentic communication.

When you embrace the Golden Rule for Communication, you listen actively and:

- pay attention and notice any emotion such as love, joy, fear, or insecurity, underneath the words you hear;
- connect to the other person's need and respond accordingly;
- confirm your connection by saying "*I hear what you say.*"

Most conflicts arise from miscommunication or misunderstandings. To limit miscommunication, be clear with your words. Focus on those words you hold as your truth and allow the other person's words to reflect his/her truth.

Treat your students and colleagues with respect and kindness, and, most likely, you will be treated in the same way. Your ability to build relationships plays a crucial role in every life you touch. Therefore, listen to others and focus on their words. Don't be afraid to ask, *"What makes you say that? I am curious to know more about your thoughts."*

DAILY PRACTICE

Discuss the Golden Rule with your students and talk about the impact it can have on the relations and communication in your class. Be aware of the way you practice the Golden Rule in communication and start using it in your classroom.

Reference to p. 233
Daily One Minute Meditation

DAY 89

VERBAL AND NON-VERBAL COMMUNICATION

Communication is made up of both verbal and non-verbal cues. Your words represent only less than 10% of what a listener gains from you. What you say matters, but your words aren't the whole picture. Your tone of voice gives the listener more than your words, close to 40%, so, how you express yourself is crucial. Together, those two factors lead to almost half of your message.

But what is the other half? It is your body language. When you walk into the classroom, be aware of your body language, the way you welcome your students and listen to the tone of your voice. It matters as much as the words you express!!! When you become aware of your verbal and non-verbal communication cues, your message will be authentic and crystal clear.

If your message and emotions are positive, it is easier for the listener to focus and understand. Your mind doesn't wander, and you stay focused. The tone of your voice and your body language produce a supportive message. You don't raise your voice, and, yet, your voice is energetic, not monotone.

If the message is negative, you may find yourself raising your voice, reaching higher pitches. Your words might become aggressive; you may lose eye-contact and your body becomes tense, closing up.

Communication patterns, as described here, may occur in your classroom. You may find yourself in different situations, when communication is positive or negative. Acknowledge and encourage the positive situations. Stop the negative situations before they escalate into a conflict.

How can you avoid negative communication? A mindful and resilient teacher recognizes the need to take action and intervenes calmly, using mindfulness practices. Breathing exercises are essential. Bring your attention to your breath, relax your face and body and move your focus away from the negative thoughts. Always control your response and take a few deep breaths before you react. Remember to count to ten before you talk.

DAILY PRACTICE

When tensions arise, you have less oxygen in your body and this brings on anxiety. The CO2 cannot be eliminated and you feel agitated. Your body is in the fight-or-flight mode.

Along with your body, your vocal cords may also be tensed and your voice will not reflect properly the message you want to send. Therefore, a breathing exercise will help relax not only your body, but your vocal cords as well. You will gain back the power of your voice and your message will be communicated in a clear and friendly manner.

The following breathing exercise can help in these situations:

- Inhale as you count to two.
- Exhale as you count to four.
- Repeat this breathing pattern for three times
- Relax your face. Start with your forehead, eyes, mouth, and jaws.
- Relax your shoulders, arms, hands, and fingers.
- Relax your chest, stomach, legs, and toes.
- Take a deep breath and continue breathing normally.
- Be confident and smile!

This body-scan type breathing exercise can help you relax and find your voice.

Reference to p. 233
Daily One Minute Meditation

DAY 90

THE AUTHENTIC VOICE OF THE TEACHER WITHIN

As you search for your *Teacher Within*, you will find that your authentic voice is part of who you are. You are aware of your words and the messages you send. You align your thoughts with your words and actions.

As a mindful and resilient teacher, you know your strengths, you acknowledge your weaknesses, and you take actions to overcome the latter. You love what you do and you don't treat your profession as a job. Even if you experience stress, you are well equipped to address it and deal with it. You smile often, make jokes, you are open to show your vulnerabilities and talk about your mistakes. You have stronger listening skills, and you are passionate about sharing your knowledge and experiences.

The authentic voice of mindful and resilient teachers is connected to their positive attitude, their speech, and in the tone and flexibility of their voice. Authentic verbal communication is also supported by non-verbal communication; together, they will make up the characteristics that define the Teacher Within. When you are aware of these characteristics and take the first actions for your personal transformation, you will notice a change in our voice and body. Your positive and supportive messages will be reflected in the eyes of the person you are talking to, and you will certainly notice the spark in their eyes. When the messages you send are negative, critical, and judgmental, the voice loses passion and enthusiasm and will be reflected in the other person's eyes with sadness and disappointment.

Mindful and resilient teachers are aware of the power of their voice and will always look for solutions to communicate authentically, to stay true to their values and avoid judgment, criticism and blame. The way we support ourselves is the way we support others. When we start to reflect on our self-talk and hear our inner voice, we will become aware of the way we speak to others and communicate our thoughts. Our inner voice is the support of our spoken voice.

DAILY PRACTICE

Over the past ten days, you have discovered your authenticity and your authentic voice. Look back and recognize your strengths and weaknesses. Be mindful and resilient as you bounce forward to support your authenticity from within.

What is the one thing you remember about these ten days?

What is the one thing you will do to strengthen your voice?

Reference to p. 233
Daily One Minute Meditation

CHAPTER TEN

EMPOWER YOUR CALLING

In this chapter, we will highlight the main concepts of this book, encouraging you to reread the ones you may need to reinforce.

Ninety days ago, you accepted our challenge to start this journey of self-discovery, to find *The Teacher Within* and empower your true calling. This search for your inner self is described in four words: Awareness, Recognition, Actions, and Transformation. This leads you to the acronym: ARAT that has become the synonym of a mindful journey towards well-being.

For any questions you might have unanswered, you can go back to the pattern of ARAT and find the solutions within yourself. Become aware of who you are, recognize your thoughts, emotions and needs, believe in your strengths and commit to actions for the desired transformation that leads to your well-being and welcomes The Teacher Within. We hope your journey with *The Teacher Within* has helped you master your thoughts and emotions, overcome your challenges with resilience, and learn how to bounce forward.

As *The Teacher Within,* you have a clear vision and aim for the ultimate goal to inspire and guide your students to find their voice, discover their spark, and make a difference in the world. The next ten days will summarize the steps you took on your journey:

- Day 91. Plant the Seeds Within
- Day 92. Awareness
- Day 93. The Link Between Your Emotions and Core Concerns
- Day 94. Follow Your Vision
- Day 95. Mental and Physical Well-Being
- Day 96. Prioritize and Accomplish Your Goals
- Day 97. Build a Safe and Nurturing Environment
- Day 98. Give Time to Others
- Day 99. Find Your Greater Purpose
- Day 100. The Door Between Your Mind and Your Heart

DAY 91

PLANT THE SEEDS WITHIN

Level One – Awareness of yourself became your first step toward your well-being. You learned how to live in the present moment, to think positive thoughts, and to bring kindness and gratitude into your life. To begin this process, you focused on your breath and practiced mindfulness.

Level Two – Recognition helped you acknowledge your thinking pattern and follow your intuition to achieve your goals. You started to understand your thoughts and emotions. You gained inner power to face your fears and worries and to recognize your strengths and weaknesses. You addressed your weaknesses and enhanced your strengths to benefit you.

Level Three – Actions showed you the path and the steps you have to take to become a mindful and resilient teacher. You went beyond academics to follow your vision, create a conscious classroom environment where you can find the genius in each student. You learned how to choose positive words of empowerment, to gain inner power and bounce forward whenever you face hardships. You embraced the need for transformation toward well-being.

Level Four – Transformation is an ongoing journey toward a state of well-being, strengthening your body, mind, and spirit, helping you to teach from the heart. You are able to embrace healthy thoughts and emotions and achieve inner peace. Your rising enthusiasm will keep your motivation alive.

At the beginning of this book, you were asked to buy seeds, like zinnias, cosmos, or marigolds. You are now ready to plant the seeds and enjoy observing the transformation they go through over the next ten days while they turn into a beautiful plant.

The Teacher Within journey itself is a holistic growth process that takes time and effort. You will reap the benefits as you enjoy the fruits of your transformational change.

DAILY PRACTICE

Take a pot with a drainage hole at the bottom. Fill it with potting soil and water it until it is moist. Plant your seeds, gently pressing it into the soil. Add water, sunlight, and love and watch your plant grow.

This process is similar to ARAT, the process of mindful growth that you have been experiencing over the past 90 days. Enjoy the beauty of who you are and watch your plant grow.

Daily One Minute Meditation

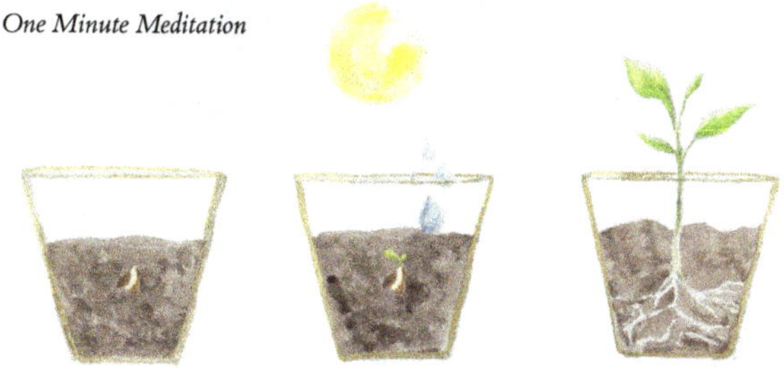

planting the seed

ONE MINUTE MEDITATION FOR CHAPTER 10

Close your eyes or lower your gaze.

Take a deep breath and release all the stress you feel now.

Focus on your breath and let all the fears
and worries leave your mind.

Bring your attention to the sound ARAT

Breathe in; breathe out and say in your mind ARAT
while you continue breathing at your normal pace.

Repeat this sound every time your mind
wanders or thinks other thoughts.

Continue saying ARAT to find the peace within.

Continue this breathing pattern for 5 minutes.

Before you open your eyes, bring your
attention to your face and smile.

Make ARAT the mantra of the Teacher Within you!

DAY 92

AWARENESS

How does awareness benefit you?

Now that you are familiar with the benefits of your awareness, you can enjoy the results. The mindfulness practices, together with the daily self-reflections and meditations, have helped you throughout this process. Place a star next to your achievements!

1. You are aware of your thoughts, words, and actions and of their impact on you and others;

2. You recognize the importance of living in the present moment, *here* and *now,* and you know how to find your peace of mind;

3. You stop and breathe, count to ten before you speak, thus opening new perspectives in your thinking process;

4. You have integrated time for yourself into your daily routine – at least five minutes a day;

5. You set your mind for a positive outcome before entering the classroom;

6. You are aware that your behavior impacts each student;

7. You are open to listen and learn from your students;

8. You create new opportunities for your students to grow;

9. You create meaningful relationships;

10. You look at each school day as a new beginning for wonderful experiences.

DAILY PRACTICE

Videotape yourself when you teach a class. Review the recording and evaluate your voice, your body language, your posture, and the emotions you reflect. Awareness of yourself is empowered by seeing yourself and imagining how this image might look to others. Your students watch you every day.

Reflect on the African proverb: "When there is no enemy within, the enemies outside can do you no harm."

Reference to p. 258
Daily One Minute Meditation

DAY 93

THE LINK BETWEEN YOUR EMOTIONS AND CORE CONCERNS

Become the manager of your emotions

Your emotions affect your mind, body, and the way you deal with your daily challenges. This has been a theme throughout this book. When you recognize your emotions, you can manage them better. You are balanced and know how to handle pressure, thus becoming more productive in your life.

Your emotions are triggered by your most important needs. Throughout the book, we address the Five Core Concerns to help you manage your emotions. We suggest you consider the following practical tools to reinforce the way you deal with your emotions based on your Core Concerns.

1. Recognize your Status and value who you are. We are all emotionally affected if our status is not appreciated or recognized.

2. Create fulfilling Roles. Identify each role you have and make them meaningful with a clear purpose.

3. Enhance Affiliation with your students and colleagues. Find those things you have in common and reduce the personal distance

when you find it appropriate. Sometimes, you need to increase affiliation and, sometimes, you need to offer space to yourself or others.

4. Show Appreciation through understanding a person's point of view; finding merit in what he/she thinks, feels, and does. Communicate your understanding through words and actions.

5. Expand your Autonomy to gain mutual benefit. Be less judgmental and take responsibility for your actions.

To reinforce the Five Core Concerns, remember the *Give Me Five* model, where each finger represents one of the concerns. It will help you manage your emotions when you understand the concern first and then the emotion connected to it. When you control your emotions, you certainly role model positive behavior to your students. They see you as an emotionally balanced person.

DAILY PRACTICE

Read again the story of the Five Core Concerns in Chapter Three and identify your current concerns. Often, we are stronger in one concern. You may find you have challenges addressing your own autonomy. It's hard for you to say *no* to someone. Or, you may find you are sensitive when your status is compromised. Be aware of the concerns most challenging to you.

Reference to p. 258
Daily One Minute Meditation

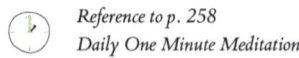

DAY 94

FOLLOW YOUR VISION

Make your vision your internal driving force.

Your vision is born from your passion, dreams, and wishes. It starts in your mind, with your thoughts and your inner voice and becomes your support to take action. Your clear vision empowers you to bounce forward when things get tough, it helps you build resilience, and you can focus on solutions instead of problems.

Your vision as a teacher is the result you want to achieve. You are dedicated and motivated to offer the best you can for your students. You have learned to define and develop your vision, thus becoming the designer of your own future. Create your vision so it encompasses your passion, dreams, and wishes. Read the following words and add to them to make them your own.

When students hear words of praise from their teacher, they learn to speak those words themselves…

When students experience inner peace in the classroom, they learn to trust themselves…

When students feel safe when they learn, they become confident and resilient…

When students model honesty from their teacher, they learn to be truthful…

When students practice mindfulness in the classroom, they learn self-awareness…

When students build a sense of community with their peers, they learn to accept others…

When teachers teach with love, their students learn to be loveable…

Mindful and resilient teachers will always recognize the most important needs of their students, guiding and inspiring them to fulfill their dreams.

DAILY PRACTICE

Create your vision. Begin by writing down five things that matter most to you and your students. Read again the words above and reflect on what matters most to you.

After you have written them down, cross out two. Keep the top three. Next, make a list of goals related to these three things that matter most. You want commit yourself to achieving your vision

Reference to p. 258
Daily One Minute Meditation

DAY 95

MENTAL AND PHYSICAL WELL-BEING

Your state of well-being impacts your students.

Your mental and physical well-being will play a crucial role in achieving your daily goals and fulfilling your vision. Paraphrasing the popular quote *"mens sana in corpore sano,"* we may think about how healthy thoughts and emotions influence our body and mind.

Your physical, social, and emotional well-being contribute to your overall health. Well-being is comprised of those factors which make your life healthy and support you so you can accomplish your dreams.

Positive routines and healthy habits included in your daily activities reduce stress, anxiety, and avoid burnout. Enhance your mental and physical well-being by creating a new approach for the Week Ahead:

Happy Monday:

- Be grateful for a new beginning and for the opportunities to learn and grow. Create a mindset that you will have a good week.
- Take a short mindful walk and focus on what you see, hear, and smell.

Mindful Tuesday:

- Make this the non-judgmental day for yourself and your students.
- Eat a piece of fruit taking mindful bites, paying attention to each bite.

Blissful Wednesday:

- Practice love and caring. The energy in the middle of the week is lowest, so boost it with acts of kindness.
- Take time to relax and make sure you get a good night's sleep.

Truthful Thursday:

- Be aware of the words you use and eliminate one word that doesn't serve you. Replace it with a positive, constructive word.
- Count the steps you take during a break and be aware that each step counts for your health.

Grateful Friday:

- Be aware and grateful for your accomplishments during the week.
- Reward yourself with something relaxing after school.

Blessed and Peaceful Weekend:

Enjoy time by yourself or with your family and friends on Saturday and Sunday.

Focus on your well-being for a life in harmony.

DAILY PRACTICE

Practice the suggested routines for the Week Ahead.

May each day count!

Reference to p. 258
Daily One Minute Meditation

DAY 96

PRIORITIZE AND ACCOMPLISH YOUR GOALS

Live your life in harmony.

You have learned to recognize the need to live in the present moment, to address your mental and physical well-being, and to cultivate a growth mindset. However, it is difficult to live in complete awareness every moment. Often, you find that your day is packed with meetings, tasks, and deadlines, and you move on autopilot, from one thing to the next, multi-tasking all day long.

When you are on autopilot, you are on high alert. You feel anxious to solve those urgent problems. Urgent matters are not always the most important ones, even though they need to be solved. Running from one urgent task to another will eventually lead to frustration and anxiety. Stop and acknowledge that it's OK if you can't accomplish it all. The skills within this book help you gain awareness of the vital matters in your life, so that you can prioritize and accomplish your goals. When you stop being on autopilot, you will save time to focus on the important things in your life and gain satisfaction. Thus, you will become proactive rather than reactive; stop judging and accept the present moment and you will set up your priorities to accomplish your tasks more efficiently.

Mindfulness practices and meditation bring your full awareness back to the *here* and *now*, so you can accomplish your vision and goals. You find time for yourself, recognizing your own meaning, learning to say *no* when it doesn't feel right, so that you can say *yes* to what feels right. You live your life in harmony, empowered by enthusiasm and motivation to teach.

DAILY PRACTICE

Make a list with those things you wish you could do but haven't found time to do them yet. Include your hobbies. Choose one and take it on. Enjoy your time doing it!

Reference to p. 258
Daily One Minute Meditation

DAY 97

BUILD A SAFE AND NURTURING ENVIRONMENT

A class with a heart enhances learning and reduces stress.

If you find harmony and motivation in your life, you teach with enthusiasm. You recognize the need to build a safe and nurturing environment for your students.

Let's reflect on the words of Carl Jung, Swiss psychologist and psychiatrist, who developed and practiced analytical psychology, "*One looks back with appreciation to the brilliant teachers, but with gratitude to those who touched our human feelings. The curriculum is so much necessary raw material, but warmth is the vital element for the growing plant and for the soul of the child.*" *The Teacher Within* guided you on your path of self-awareness to find the warmth within and project it on your students. As a mindful and resilient teacher, you are authentic, you teach from your heart and go beyond academics to enhance learning. Make your presence count and give the best you can. There is always more in you than you think. Consider each class an opportunity to grow both for you and your students.

Your responsibility is to encourage your students every day. Be present, make them feel appreciated, and build healthy relationships based on meaningful communication. Set up positive routines and create a positive atmosphere of confidence and trust that enhances your teaching. Use a *good day's* mindset for every class you teach. Start with a smile on your face when you enter the classroom; a smile sends the message of love, care, and trust. It has the power of letting your students know they are in a safe, warm, and caring environment where learning can be interesting and fun. It sets up the tone for the entire class, no matter how challenging it might be.

Continue your class with words of encouragement, acknowledging your students' strengths and see the genius in each and every one of them. End your day with a positive tone and don't forget to smile before you leave the classroom. This may be the only act of kindness some of your students will receive during the day. Be aware that you, the teacher, can touch the soul of every student.

DAILY PRACTICE

Read again Carl Jung's words and reflect on how you touch your students' human feelings every day?

Write your statement about how you would like your students to remember you in ten years from now. Would you be one of those teachers they remember in 20 years from now?

Reference to p. 258
Daily One Minute Meditation

DAY 98

GIVE TIME TO OTHERS

Extend your class with a heart beyond the walls of your classroom.

When you are aware of yourself and live in the *here* and *now*, you teach from your heart. You serve your students, you teach, support and help them grow. You find joy in teaching and your willingness to share this joy with others increases. Your teaching goes beyond your classroom. You might find yourself taking extra time to support students who need more attention, or colleagues who need your experience and expertise. You may even consider taking time for charitable projects to serve others outside of your school.

Your time gains special value and you share it with kindness and love. The best gift you can give others is your time; you'll never get it back, but it will leave its imprint on them. A shared experience is an enhanced experience – share your time and you will feel richer than ever. This gives meaning to your life.

There are people who will benefit from who you are and what you can give. If you engage in a meaningful act of service, you will keep your health and well-being connected. Think about who needs you and how you can help them. Remember the Chinese proverb: *"If you want happiness for a lifetime, help somebody else."*

DAILY PRACTICE

What can you do today? Spend five minutes serving someone. Then ask yourself, *"How do I feel?"*

Reference to p. 258
Daily One Minute Meditation

DAY 99

FIND YOUR GREATER PURPOSE

Teaching is a profession with a calling and a great purpose.

We started this journey with the end in mind: to help you find the *Teacher Within*, a mindful and resilient professional with a vision and a meaningful life. Throughout the book, you learned new concepts and reinforced the ones you knew already. You became aware of yourself, recognized your thoughts, emotions, strengths, and needs. You understood your authentic voice has to be honest and filled with respect and responsibility to best influence the lives of your students.

We all search for a meaningful life filled with happiness and satisfaction and a purpose that gives us the driving force to go on and succeed. Where do you find meaning each day? What do you want to accomplish? What actions are most important to you?

When your life has a direction, supported by your purpose and vision, you know why you get out of bed every morning and go to school. Teaching is a meaningful profession with a great purpose. *The Teacher Within* is who you are or what you can become.

DAILY PRACTICE

Think of a teacher who inspired you and influenced your life.

What do you think his/her greater purpose was?

Reflect on your own purpose in life and write it down as a statement.

Reference to p. 258
Daily One Minute Meditation

DAY 100

THE DOOR BETWEEN YOUR MIND AND YOUR HEART

Your vision is clear when you open the door between your mind and your heart.

We often say "*the longest journey one will ever take is the 14 inch journey from the mind to the heart*." When you open the door to your heart, you feel love, empathy, and compassion toward yourself and others. You have a meaningful life and your vision becomes your lighthouse.

Your journey started with courage and curiosity and it took commitment to get here, on Day 100. You have gone through many days of reflection and self-discovery while you learned how the process of ARAT connects the wisdom of your mind with the wisdom of your heart. This journey of genuine transformation opened the door between your mind and your heart. If you continue to live with the awareness of your body and senses, while you recognize and accept the thoughts and emotions and take actions with gratefulness from your heart, your spiritual transformation will help you blossom at your fullest potential. You will experience the meaningful life of The Teacher Within.

As you turn the last page of your journey, you may realize this is not the end but rather a new beginning for you as a mindful, resilient, and authentic teacher.

DAILY PRACTICE

MEDITATION

Make yourself comfortable and settle in for meditation.

Close your eyes or lower your gaze.

Focus on your breath and believe in yourself and the peace you have within.

Bring your attention to the sound **ARAT**.

Repeat the word as you keep your attention focused on this sound.

Allow your body to relax.

Breathe in; breathe out and say in your mind **ARAT**, while you continue breathing at your normal pace.

Continue saying **ARAT** to find the peace within.

Repeat this sound every time your mind wanders or thinks other thoughts.

Allow the sound of **ARAT** to enter your heart.

Imagine **ARAT** as the key that opens the door between your mind and your heart.

Feel your whole body relaxed and embrace the spirit of transformation.

Make **ARAT** your mantra while you welcome the authentic Teacher Within you!

Smile as you slowly open your eyes.

APPRECIATION

TO DR. DANIEL SHAPIRO

A deep note of gratitude to Harvard Professor Daniel L. Shapiro, recognized throughout the world for his contributions in the field of negotiation. We draw heavily on his 'core concerns framework' for addressing emotions in everyday interactions and highly recommend you read his book, ***Beyond Reason: Using Emotions As You Negotiate***. Thank you, Dan, for enriching our book by offering teachers a unique method to understand more about themselves and their students.

TO RUXANDRA MERCEA

Our gratitude extends to Ruxandra Mercea, for her continuous support and encouragement as the Executive Director of Transylvania College, inspirational teacher, and Simona and Dan's daughter. She had the chance to grow up with the school founded by her parents, to witness all the changes, and learn from her experience. Today, Ruxandra is a young, visionary leader, committed to make a difference and to improve education in Romania.

ACKNOWLEDGEMENTS

We have worked and developed many projects together over the past 25 years and this book has been in the making for more than five years. However, writing *The Teacher Within* has been an entirely different experience - an intensive, yet meaningful and fun experience for the two of us. Along the way, we learned a lot from each other. Nevertheless, as two writers from different backgrounds, American and Romanian, the communication in English not only challenged us but also made us recognize and embrace the differences in our cultures. Ultimately, we managed to get to a universal understanding that we, as human beings, are more similar than we are different. We hope our readers gain from what we have achieved through this process. The path has been amazing for both of us and we thank all those who guided us along our way. We feel blessed to have had the support of an amazing community of family, friends, and colleagues.

COMMUNITY OF COLLEAGUES

The Teacher Within would not have been possible without the insight, knowledge and commitment of the teachers who shared their stories with us. We are grateful for all the lessons we learned from them and for their dedication to the teaching profession. This book would have never had the depth and realistic scenarios without their contribution.

Special acknowledgements and appreciation to all the teachers at Transylvania College. They have been instrumental in their insights and their allegiance to *The Teacher Within*. We extend our gratitude to the entire community of Transylvania College for their support, inspiration, and guidance.

Words of gratitude to:

Ana-Maria Huluban, a media studies teacher and amazing artist, for the wonderful visual representation of the concepts presented in this book, as well as *The Teacher Within* logo.

Zsuzsa Magyary, for all the time we worked together, sharing with us her professional expertise and technical support day by day, being an inspiration for each of us. Working together brought us closer and we developed a meaningful friendship.

Corina Chiorean, for her gentle and professional guidance. When we felt that everything was falling apart, she was there to support us and keep all of us connected and organized.

Harry Shuttleworth, Director of Staff Development, who brought along his international and professional expertise.

Delia Filipescu, Lavinia Ungureanu, Simina Bejenaru, Iulia Bratfalean-Igna, Ciprian Ghisa, Cristina Ungvari, Daniela Preda, Dorina Girbovan, Mihaela Romaniuc, Virgil Ganea, Cosmina Mocanu, Claudia Eli, Erika Farkas, Laura Tatar, Melinda Szalontai, Ioana Balint, Raluca Lenarth, Ana-Maria Nasui, Raluca Stoenoiu, Adina Toma, Lavinia Ungureanu, and all the teachers who have been working enthusiastically with us over the years, accepting the challenge to pioneer a new approach for education in Romania.

Paul Kennedy, Jeannette Jones and Daniel Philips for bringing along their international teaching expertise.

Anca Rusu, Andra Sfetcu, Catrinel Grigorovici, and Domnita Fechete who are always ready to support, encourage, and share good practices at Transylvania College.

We extend our gratitude to the Parent Community for their wisdom and valuable suggestions. Thanks to Lilia Dicu, Mihaela Miron, Monica Suciu, Delia Rus, S.P. O'Mahony.

Smriti Menon Chatterji, for her guidance and support. Her input is greatly appreciated; she gave us honest and solid critique to improve the outcome. Her ability to work with us on SKYPE, through email, and often late into the night crafting words with a deft touch will never be forgotten. Your organizational guidance has provided a solid foundation to this book.

Our broader community from across the globe.

Cristina Marine for her superb editing skills and the countless hours she spent to ensure the consistency of the text. She has a special talent as an editor, with a focus on balanced sentences incorporating the authors' cultural differences. Her ability to work with Susan in the United States and Simona in Romania was a special gift. We thank you wholeheartedly!

A special thank you to Claudia Rosales who gave us her time, helped with the meditations, created a mindfulness and acting program in the hills of Transylvania, and shared her passion to help teachers become mindful and more compassionate.

Joan Myhre, teacher, friend, and colleague who shared her wisdom over and over again and is one of the best teachers ever. Her ability to express the teachers' needs is remarkable.

Joan's grandson, Eli Conniff, a very special thank you, for allowing us to tell your story of resilience. You are truly a model of resilience for us.

Amy Dixon who offered invaluable support through her knowledge of mindfulness and meditation practices. And thank you Amy for taking Susan's picture at the Skyhouse Yoga Center.

Vera Janikova and Ivan Janik for their love, support, and for reading several drafts of this book. They believe in *The Teacher Within* and offer their own workshops with similar messages throughout the Czech Republic.

Nathan and Fian Pacey from Hong Kong, for our shared passion for education and for their confidence and trust in *The Teacher Within*.

On behalf of Simona, we wish to extend our gratitude to Lucinda and Alexander Scott, the first who trusted and encouraged her, offering their unconditional support over the years.

We express our appreciation to the international teachers and heads of schools from all over the world. It was a privilege to learn from the best! Special thanks to Peter Pelham, founder of Global Connections, who encouraged Simona to follow and accomplish her vision in education. A warm thank you to all her friends and colleagues from Global Connections, Round Square, COBIS and Leader in Me.

COMMUNITY OF REVIEWERS

International scholars and practitioners critically reviewed *The Teacher Within* and provided detailed, insightful feedback:

Dr. Mira Polazarevska, Skopje, Macedonia, for constantly reminding us that psychological health is an integral dimension of the text. Through her teachings, particularly to Susan, she contributed great insight for this text.

Clare King contributed to several drafts, adding her expertise as a peer counselor at Johns Hopkins University, MD, USA.

Dr. Peter Killeen, Police Psychologist, who has reviewed the content, together with Susan, and showed unwavering enthusiasm for the concepts of mindfulness and resilience. He helped us define life's purpose and allowed us to reference his book, Operation Longevity, co-authored by Susan Shapiro.

Anushka Maroli, international consultant, for her broad lifetime educational experiences in schools in Thailand and India. Thank you for your review of the material and your belief in this book.

THE PUBLISHING COMMUNITY

Writing a book is one thing; making the format match these ideas is another story. Our gratitude to Mihaela Miron for turning our into a beautiful book filled with colors, pictures, and love and to the Studio Impress Design Printing House in Cluj-Napoca. Special thanks to Mihai-Vlad Guta for his inspired layout.

OUR SACRED COMMUNITY

We want to thank our husbands whose patience and love gave us hope when we were exhausted and on our umpteenth draft! Ronnie and Dan, you are our daily inspiration.

A warm thank you to all of our children who have taught us and continue to teach us more than anyone on earth. To Steve and Shira, Dan and Mia, Maddie and Mike, Ruxandra and Voicu, Tudor and Silvia, you are our special gifts in life. We are thankful for all you have given us.

To our grandchildren who are our future: Noah, Jake, Zachary, Annie, Liam, Ilinca, Petra, Vlad.

A special note of gratitude from Susan to her sisters, two special women, Margaret Gold and Elizabeth Sealey, who provided constant support and recommendations throughout our writing journey. We appreciate your help, your love, and your constant support, never giving up on the two of us, ever!

A special thought of gratitude from Simona to her parents, Livia and Dumitru Pop, for being the first ones to try breathing and meditation practices mentioned in the book. Special thanks to her sister, Roxana Jaeger Gassert, for all the meaningful lessons learned from her and for her patience to listen all the time.

And, finally, we extend our gratitude to you, the reader. For your faith in choosing this book and allowing us to be part of your life-journey in a small way. Thank you.

REFERENCES

Nguyen Anh-Huong and Thich Nhat Hanh (2006) **Walking Meditation**; Sounds True, Inc. Boulder, Colorado

Anne Marie Albano, Ph.D (2013) **You and Your Anxious Child: Free from Fears and Worries and Create a Joyful Family Life;** Penguin Press

Elaine N. Aron, Ph.D (2000) **The Highly Sensitive Person**; Broadway Books

Mitch Albom (2012) **The Time Keeper**; Hyperion Press

Susan L. Barrett (1992) **It's ALL in your HEAD**; Free Spirit; Revised, Updated edition

Tony Buzan (2002) **HEAD FIRST: 10 Ways to Tap into your Natural Genius**; Thorsons, an imprint of HarperCollins Publishers

Renee Baron and Elizabeth Wagele, (1994) **The Enneagram Made Easy: Discover the 9 Types of People**; Harper, San Francisco

Jim Bagnola (2012) **Becoming a Professional Human Being**; Global Thinking Press

Rudolph M. Ballentine (1987) **The Theory and Practice of Meditation;** Himalayan Inst Pr; Revised, Expanded, Subsequent edition

Shelley Carson, Ph.D. (2010) **Your Creative Brain: Seven Steps to Maximize Imagination, Productivity, and Innovation in Your Life**; Jossey-Bass; 1 edition

Charles Duhigg (2012) **The Power of Habit: Why We Do What We Do in Life and Business–,** Random House Trade Paperbacks, New York

Dr. Wayne W. Dyer (2004) **The Power of Intention: Learning to Co-create Your World Your Way**; Hay House

Roger Fisher and Daniel Shapiro (2006) **Beyond Reason: Using Emotions as You Negotiate**; Penguin Books; 1 edition

Roger Fisher and Scott Brown (1988) **Getting Together: Building Relationships as We Negotiate**; Penguin Books

Roger Fisher, William L. Ury and Bruce Patton (1991) **Getting To Yes: Negotiating Agreement Without Giving In;** Penguin Books; Revised edition

Mari Fitzduff (1988) **Community Conflict Skills: A Handbook for Group Work in Northern Irelan**d; Express Litho, Belfast

Elaine Fox (2012) **Rainy Brain, Sunny Brain: The New Science of Optimism and Pessimism;** Arrow Books

Jenny Friedman, Ph.D. Jolene Roehlkepartain (2010) **Doing Good Together: 101 Easy, Meaningful Service Projects for Families, Schools and Communities**; Free Spirit Publishing

Howard Gardner (2006) **Multiple Intelligences: New Horizons in Theory and Practice**; Basic Books; Reprint edition

Daniel Goleman (2015) **A Force for Good: The Dalai Lama's Vision for Our World;** Bantam, First Edition edition

Daniel Goleman (2014) **What Makes a Leader: Why Emotional Intelligence Matters;** More Than Sound

Thich Nhat Hanh (2012) **Fear: Essential Wisdom for Getting Through the Storm**; Harper One

Timber Hawkeye (2013) **Buddhist Boot Camp**; HarperCollins

Cheri Huber (1990) **That Which You are Seeking is Causing You to Seek**; Keep It Simple Books; 1st Edition

Gerald G. Jampolsky (1979) **Love is Letting Go of Fear**; M.D. Celestial Arts, Berkeley, CA

Gerri Johnson, Gershen Kaufman, Ph.D. and Lev Raphael, Ph.D. (1991) **Stick Up for Yourself: A 10 Part Course in Self-Esteem and Assertiveness for Kids**; Free Spirit Publishing

Gary Khor (2004) **Reflections on Qi: Turning Your Life to the World's Hidden Energy**; New Holland Publishers, Australia

Jonni Kincher (1995) **Psychology for Kids**; Free Spirit Publishing

Jonni Kincher (1995) **Psychology for Kids II**; Free Spirit Publishing

Daniel Kahneman, (2012) **Thinking Fast and Slow**; Penguin Books

Anya Kamenet (2010) **Edupunks, Edupreneurs, and the Coming Transformation of Higher Education;** Chelsea Green Publishing, White River Junction, Vermont

Tom Kelley and David Kelley (2013) **Creative Confidence: Unleashing the Creative Potential within Us All**; Crown Business; 1 edition

Dalai Lama (2007) **The Universe in a Single Atom: The Convergence of Science and Spirituality;** Three Rivers Press

Hugh L. Levin (2011) **The Saying of Buddha** – Journal, LLC 2011

Robert Maurer, Ph.D (2004) **One Small Step Can Change Your Life – The Kaizen Way**; Workman Publishing, New York

Alexander D. Platt, Caroline E. Tripp, Wayne R. Ogden, and Robert G. Fraser (2000) **The Skillful Leader: Confronting Mediocre Teaching**; Ready About Press

Parker J. Palmer (2009), **A Hidden Wholeness: The Journey Toward an Undivided Life;** Jossey-Bass

Dr. Norman Vincent Peale (1993) **Positive Thinking Every Day: An Inspiration for Each Day of the Year;** Touchstone; 1 edition

Helen Palmer (1991) **Enneagram: Understanding Yourself and the Others in Your Life**; Harper Collins

David Richo (2006) **The Five Things We Cannot Change ...and the Happiness We Find by Embracing Them**; Shambalah Publications, Boston and London

Geshe Sonam Rinchen (1997) **The Thirty-Seven Practices of Bodhisattvas: An Oral Teaching**; Snow Lion Publications; Ithaca, New York

Ken Robinson (2011) **Out of Our Minds: Learning to be Creative**; Capstone Publishing

David Richo (2002) **How to Be an Adult in Relationships: The Five Keys to Mindful Loving**; Shambalah, Boston and London

Don Richard Riso (1989) **Personality Types: Using the Enneagram for Self-Discovery**; Houghton-Mifflin

Daniel L. Shapiro (2016) **Negotiating the Nonnegotiable: How to Resolve Your Most Emotionally Charged Conflicts**; Viking Press, Penguin Books

Daniel Shapiro (2004) **Conflict and Communication: A Guide through the Labyrinth of Conflict Management**; International Debate Education Association

Daniel L. Shapiro (Editor), Brooke E. Clayton (Editor), Roger Fisher (Foreword by) (2004) **New Directions for Youth Development: Negotiation, Interpersonal Approaches to Intergroup Conflict**; Jossey-Bass; 1 edition

Daniel Shapiro (2004) **Conflict and Communication: A Guide through the Labyrinth of Conflict Management**; International Debate Education Association

Daniel L. Shapiro (Editor), Brooke E. Clayton (Editor), Roger Fisher (Foreword by) (2004) **New Directions for Youth Development: Negotiation, Interpersonal Approaches to Intergroup Conflict**; Jossey-Bass; 1 edition

Daniel L. Shapiro (2016) **Negotiating the Nonnegotiable: How to Resolve Your Most Emotionally Charged Conflicts**; Viking Press, Penguin Books

Tara Singh (1989) **Nothing Real Can Be Threatened: Exploring a Course in Miracles**; Life Action Press, Los Angeles

David Stoop (2003) **You Are What You Think**; Revell; Reprint edition

Don L. Sorenson, Ph.D (1992) **Conflict Resolution and Mediation for Peer Helpers**; Educational Media Corporation

Shel Silverstein (2006) **The Missing Piece**; Harper & Row

Shel Silverstein (2006) **The Missing Piece Meets the Big O**; Harper & Row

Susan Shapiro (2012) **The Butterfly Club** – a compilation of children's stories for her five grandchildren

Douglas Stone, Bruce Patton and Sheila Heen (2010) **Difficult Conversations: How to Discuss What Matters Most**; Penguin Books; Anniversary, Updated edition

Mel Silberman (1990) **Active Training: A Handbook of Techniques, Designs, Case Examples and Tips**; Lexington Books

Harry Stein (1982) **Ethics (and Other Liabilities): Trying to Live Right in an Amoral World**; St. Martin's Press, New York

Helen Schucman and William Thetford (1976) **A Course in Miracles**; Foundation for Inner Peace

John Teasdale, Mark Williams, Zindel Segal (2014) **The Mindful Way Workbook: An 8-Week Program to Free Yourself from Depression and Emotional Distress**; The Guilford Press

Eckhart Tolle (2004) **Stillness Speaks**; Pgw,

Iyanla Vanzant (2013) **Forgiveness: 21 Days to Forgive Everyone for Everything**; Smiley Books

Ajahn Brahm Venerable (2015) **Opening the Door of Your Heart: And Other Buddhist Tales of Happiness**; Hachette Australia

Mark Williams and Danny Penman (2011) Mindfulness: **An Eight-Week Plan for Finding Peace in a Frantic World**; Rodale Books

Edie West (1999) **The Big Book of Icebreakers: Quick, Fun Activities for Energizing Meetings and Workshops**; McGraw Hill

EBOOKS:

Helen Palmer (1994) **The Enneagram Study Guide**; HarperCollins Publisher, 1994

OTHER PUBLICATIONS:

Adventures in Parenting: How Responding, Preventing, Monitoring and Modeling Can Help You Become a Successful Parent -US Dept. of Health and Human Services, National Institute of Health, Eunice Kennedy Shriver National Institute of Child Health and Human Development

How to Make Supervision and Evaluation Really Work: Supervision and Evaluation in the Context of Strengthening School Culture – Jon Saphier, Research for Better Teaching, Inc. One Acton Place, Acton, Massachusetts, 1993

The MindUP Curriculum: Brain Focused Strategies for Learning – and Living, Scholastic The Hawn Foundation, 2011

Dilemmas of Diversity: Analyses of "Cultural Difference" by U.S. and Russia-Based Scholars, Woodrow Wilson International Center for Scholars, Kennan Institute – Michele Rivkin-Fish and Elena Trubina, 2010 Washington DC

Occupational Athlete System: Your Personal Game Plan – Interactive Health and Safety System, Susan Shapiro. Occupational Athletics Health and Safety Systems, LLC. 2016

State, Society, and Transformation, Edited by Beth A. Mitchneck, Woodrow Wilson International Center for Scholars, Kennan Institute, 2011

Domino: All Different, All Equal – A Manual to use Peer Group Education as a Means to Fight Racism, Xenophobia, Anti-Semitism and Intolerance, Council of Europe, Strasbourg, France, 1993

The Skillful Teacher: Building Your Teaching Skills – Jon Saphier, Robert Gower, Research for Better Teaching, Inc. Acton, MA 1997

BOOKS BY SUSAN SHAPIRO

Operation Longevity: A Mindful Approach to Wellness and Resilience for Law Enforcement Professionals in the 21st Century, co-author with Dr. Peter Killeen, 2018 specifically for law enforcement officers or federal agents. With an accompanying Personal Journal, these two books enable these professionals to live a healthy, happy, and sustainable life while working in the law enforcement field and through their retirement years.

The Curtain Rises: Oral Histories of the Fall of Communism in Eastern Europe. Published by McFarland Publishers in 2004._www.mcfarlandpub.com, this book tells the stories of extraordinary people, how they lived under Communism and how life has changed since the fall of the wall.

Life Skills Training for AmeriCorps includes career management, mindfulness, time management, attitude and happiness, conflict and communication, nutrition, stress management, motivation, and disease prevention. (2010)

Health education curricula and training guides for the Open Society Foundation Health Education Program for kindergarten through high school students on:

- Nutrition for Students
- Smoking Prevention
- Alcohol and Other Drugs
- Environment and Our Global World

Conflict and Communication: A Guide Through the Labyrinth of Conflict Management (Ed.), translated into 27 languages and implemented in schools within the United

States and across Eastern and Central Europe and Central Asia.

Subcontracting Peace, The Challenges of NGO Peacebuilding, Edited by Oliver P. Richmond and Henry F. Carey. ***The Challenges of an NGO in Post-Communist Europe: Contributing author. The Open Society Health Education Program***. ASHGATE Publishers 2005.

Peer mediation and training curriculum for teachers, school principals and health and wellness educators from six countries implemented in schools in the following countries. Greece, Belgium, Italy, Slovenia, Lithuania and Estonia; July, 2005.

Three year long student planners for middle school students in Pennsylvania to address the issues of childhood obesity and lifestyle changes.

A Parent Supplement to the Student Planners, gives parents suggestions to discuss the planners with their children and implement the changes within their family.

Pen Pals for Peace, a collection of drawings and letters written by children living in Sarajevo during the siege of that city when its residents were under constant bombardment and sniper fire. Writing to pen pals in America, the children tell extraordinary stories about their experiences of the war amidst the ordinary preoccupations of childhood.

The Road Athlete System (revised edition, 2016) and ***The Bus Athlete System, (2005),*** address the health and safety concerns within the transportation industry. Each system includes an interactive book and CDs. Each book has a twelve month plan designed to make simple changes in drivers' health and safety. The systems are based on twelve lifestyle factors: Nutrition, Physical Exercise, Mental Fitness, Stress Reduction, Attitude and Happiness, Sleep and Fatigue, Substance Abuse, Time Management, Motivation, Disease Prevention, Weight Control, and Relaxation Techniques.

Six Training Modules (350 pages) designed to instruct safety trainers in ***The Road Athlete System***. Written for trainers to teach the ***Road Athlete System***, the series also helps the trainers develop their training skills.

The Occupational Athlete System second edition (2016), written for working environments, and consists of an interactive book, a twelve month plan to help people make simple changes in their health and safety.

The Butterfly Club, a book for young children filled with stories building character and mindfulness.

AUTHOR BIOGRAPHY – SUSAN SHAPIRO

Ms. Susan Shapiro is an author, motivational speaker, education and training specialist with comprehensive experience in teaching, teacher training, curriculum development and programming. She has designed, developed and implemented life skills training programs for students and adults that have impacted the teaching and training of educators in thousands of schools across the globe. She is co- authoring a book with Dr. Peter Killeen, law enforcement professional on mindfulness, resilience and well-being, **Operation Longevity: A Mindful Approach to Wellness and Resilience for Law Enforcement in the 21st Century**. Susan Shapiro has published a book with McFarland Publishers, **The Curtain Rises: Oral Histories of the Fall of Communism in Eastern Europe**. She has also written her memoir, **The Perseverance of Hope,** her personal story comparing cultures in different countries. Her training materials, books, curricula, and student planners are used world-wide in schools, libraries, and universities.

AUTHOR BIOGRAPHY - SIMONA BACIU

Simona Baciu is an innovative and visionary leader in education. She is a recipient of the British International School Lifetime Award and holder of the Custodian of the Romanian Crown Medal, awarded for her outstanding contribution to education.

At the beginning of the 1990's, as a teacher in a state school in Romania, Simona decided to start a school that would introduce change in the prevailing system and make a difference in the lives of students. Happy Kids Kindergarten was opened in 1993 in one of the rooms of her family's small apartment. This is how Transylvania College, today a well-known and prestigious institution with over 700 students, was born.

Simona is an educator, speaker, author, trainer, and consultant for the improvement of education in Romania and abroad. As a Board Member of Round Square, Global Connections, Princess Margareta of Romania Foundation, and TedX Eroilor, Simona acts as a global agent of change for education. She has authored numerous articles and spoken at both national and international events and conferences promoting education for the 21st century, incorporating social-emotional learning, mindfulness, and well-being.

Simona believes that education should cultivate and nurture a love for life-long learning in everyone, while keeping a curious mind, an open heart and a caring soul for the world in which we live.

www.ingramcontent.com/pod-product-compliance
Lightning Source LLC
Chambersburg PA
CBHW060125130626
46556CB00006B/2241
* 9 7 9 8 9 8 6 0 5 7 4 2 2 *